Cambridge Elements

Elements in Current Archaeological Tools and Techniques
edited by
Hans Barnard
Cotsen Institute of Archaeology
Willeke Wendrich
Polytechnic University of Turin

ARCHAEOASTRONOMY

Data Collection and Analysis

A. César González-García
Institute of Heritage Sciences (INCIPIT) – Spanish National Research Council (CSIC)

COTSEN INSTITUTE OF
ARCHAEOLOGY AT UCLA

CAMBRIDGE
UNIVERSITY PRESS

Shaftesbury Road, Cambridge CB2 8EA, United Kingdom

One Liberty Plaza, 20th Floor, New York, NY 10006, USA

477 Williamstown Road, Port Melbourne, VIC 3207, Australia

314–321, 3rd Floor, Plot 3, Splendor Forum, Jasola District Centre, New Delhi – 110025, India

Cambridge University Press is part of Cambridge University Press & Assessment, a department of the University of Cambridge.

We share the University's mission to contribute to society through the pursuit of education, learning and research at the highest international levels of excellence.

www.cambridge.org
Information on this title: www.cambridge.org/9781009639361
DOI: 10.1017/9781009639316

© A. César González-García 2026

This publication is in copyright. Subject to statutory exception and to the provisions of relevant collective licensing agreements, no reproduction of any part may take place without the written permission of Cambridge University Press & Assessment.

When citing this work, please include a reference to the DOI 10.1017/9781009639316

First published 2026

A catalogue record for this publication is available from the British Library

A Cataloging-in-Publication data record for this Element is available from the Library of Congress

ISBN 978-1-009-63936-1 Hardback
ISBN 978-1-009-63935-4 Paperback
ISSN 2632-7031 (online)
ISSN 2632-7023 (print)

Additional resources for this publication at: www.cambridge.org/GonzálezGarcía

Cambridge University Press & Assessment has no responsibility for the persistence or accuracy of URLs for external or third-party internet websites referred to in this publication and does not guarantee that any content on such websites is, or will remain, accurate or appropriate.

For EU product safety concerns, contact us at Calle de José Abascal, 56, 1°, 28003 Madrid, Spain, or email eugpsr@cambridge.org

Archaeoastronomy

Data Collection and Analysis

Elements in Current Archaeological Tools and Techniques

DOI: 10.1017/9781009639316
First published online: March 2026

A. César González-García
Institute of Heritage Sciences (INCIPIT) – Spanish National Research Council (CSIC)
Author for correspondence: A. César González-García,
a.cesar.gonzalez-garcia@incipit.csic.es

Abstract: How does archaeoastronomy assist archaeologists in comprehending the past of human societies? Archaeoastronomy is an interdisciplinary field that combines scientific principles and astronomical measurements to enhance our understanding of ancient cultures. Its interdisciplinary character appears by blending areas of the natural sciences, such as astronomy, physics, mathematics, and even geology or biology, with others of the social sciences and humanities, such as archaeology, history, prehistory, geography, or anthropology. Throughout this Element we are going to see what archaeoastronomy is about, how it works, and what topics it is applied to, for which we are going to introduce a series of concepts from astronomy, mathematics, and other disciplines.

Keywords: archaeoastronomy, cultural astronomy, data gathering, solar orientations, lunar orientations

© A. César González-García 2026

ISBNs: 9781009639361 (HB), 9781009639354 (PB), 9781009639316 (OC)
ISSNs: 2632-7031 (online), 2632-7023 (print)

Contents

	Introduction	1
1	What Is Archaeoastronomy: Astronomy in Culture	1
2	How Archaeoastronomy Works: Data Gathering	5
3	Positional Astronomy	17
4	Movements of the Sun	23
5	Movements of the Moon	31
6	Calendars	37
7	Eclipses and the Cycles of the Moon	40
8	The Planets	43
9	The Stars	46
10	Other Ways of Measuring Orientations	56
11	Precision versus Accuracy and Error Analysis	70
12	Conclusion	79
	References	81

Introduction

How does archaeoastronomy assist archaeologists in comprehending the past of human societies? As we will insist in this Element, archaeoastronomy is an interdisciplinary field that combines scientific principles and astronomical measurements to enhance our understanding of ancient cultures. Its interdisciplinary character appears by blending areas of the natural sciences, such as astronomy, physics, mathematics, and even geology or biology, with others of the social sciences and humanities, such as archaeology, history, prehistory, geography, or anthropology.

Throughout this Element we are going to see what archaeoastronomy is about, how it works, and what topics it is applied to, for which we are going to introduce a series of concepts from astronomy, mathematics, or other disciplines.

1 What Is Archaeoastronomy: Astronomy in Culture

For most of human history, the sky among many other things was a tool. Its regularities helped define calendars and helped humans orient themselves in journeys over long distances. Humans situate themselves in space and time thanks to points of reference. New Year's Day or the day we first see the lunar crescent can be used to define beginnings in a new cycle that allows us to mark the times of the calendar. In the same way, to situate ourselves in the landscape, we depend on the sky. For example, directions on Earth acquire their meaning from where the Sun rises or sets.

Nowadays, *astronomy* is a word that is loaded with scientific weight. We understand astronomy as the science of the heavens. However, I'd like to delve a little into the etymology of the word *astronomy*. Indeed it is formed by the Greek words *astro*, meaning star, and *nomo* or *nomoi*. This last includes the concept of law, so astronomy would be the laws of the heavenly bodies, and as such was used and understood in antiquity alongside astrology. However, *nomoi* could also be the cultural uses and customs associated with something. In that sense, then, astronomy could naturally be understood as the customs and social uses associated with the sky. And this is a very fit definition for cultural astronomy and archaeoastronomy, as we will see.

Archaeoastronomy is the scientific discipline that is dedicated to unraveling and understanding the worldview and cultural uses of astronomical phenomena among prehistoric peoples, ancient cultures, and current non-Western societies. In this way, archaeoastronomy is our tool to know how the people who built the megaliths or the ancient Egyptians or the cultures of Mesoamerica interacted with the heavens.

In a more rigorous definition, archaeoastronomy is a highly interdisciplinary line of research that deals with the study of prehistoric, ancient, and traditional astronomy within the framework of its cultural context (Ruggles 2011). Archaeoastronomy therefore covers the following topics: calendars; practical observation; celestial cults and myths; symbolic representation of astronomical events, concepts, and objects; astronomical orientation of tombs, temples, sanctuaries, and urban centers; traditional cosmology; and the ceremonial application of astronomical traditions (Krupp 1997).

This is a discipline that, from different points of view, complements and deepens the knowledge obtained from other disciplinary orientations such as landscape archaeology, understanding it broadly; the history of religions, considering everything from the orientation of sacred places to the ritual conditions that govern calendars; and historical anthropology, conceived as an approach to the study of the conceptions of the cosmos that are raised in different cultures. In addition, archaeoastronomy can be understood as a part of the history of science since it investigates the knowledge of the cosmos that is achieved in different cultures and historical periods.

In this Element we are going to focus above all on a specific aspect of archaeoastronomy, which is ultimately the one that defines it in its essence, which is the measure of orientations of architectural structures, tombs, buildings, or sanctuaries in relation to the landscape.

Throughout history, human knowledge has often been specialized. Individuals may dedicate significant portions of their time to specific tasks or fields, such as ritual practices, medicine, astronomy, and more. However, such science is conducted within the society where it is produced, as stated by neuroscientist Marcus Jacobson (1993). Exploring the social aspect of this knowledge raises questions, data, and methods that extend beyond a specialist's expertise. A comprehensive social and human interpretation of this knowledge is required to address these questions. Regarding the study of the sky, such an approach is referred to as cultural astronomy (González-García & Belmonte 2019; González-García 2024).

Cultural astronomy examines how historical and prehistoric societies relate to the sky they lived under. As such, it belongs to the part of the humanities that focuses on the influence of the environment on human societies and is far from a specialized archaeometry or an extension of the history of astronomy.

Astronomers might be interested in understanding what past societies observed in the sky. However, cultural astronomers and archaeoastronomers seek to comprehend how these societies generated, processed, and utilized their astronomical knowledge. Thus the emphasis is not on the celestial objects identified by these societies, but rather on how those observations were interpreted and integrated into their cultural framework.

Stanislaw Iwaniszewski (2009) defines cultural astronomy as the study of the relations between people's perception of the sky and the organization of different aspects of social life. Cultural astronomy thus seeks to understand how ancient, traditional, and ancestral societies produced astronomical knowledge. How was this knowledge passed down? Were processes of social production, transfer, and diffusion involved? Did all societies independently develop such knowledge, or were key principles like solstices and equinoxes shared between cultures? Were early astronomers a distinct social group, or did they have privileged status? Or was astronomy knowledge more general with no specific authors? Additionally, what impact did the concept of the sky have on power dynamics and societal structures?

Such study, according to Edwin Krupp (1997), includes several different topics including the ritualized representation of astronomical events, for instance in dance or pilgrimages or the relationship between music and astronomy.

Cultural astronomy includes several other subdisciplines, such as ethnoastronomy and astronomy in traditional and subsidiary societies (like pastoral and nomadic groups), and archaeoastronomy. Archaeoastronomy commonly refers to the examination of the orientation of built structures and the characteristics of landscapes in relation to astronomical phenomena, but it also deals with mobile artifacts, carved bones, stones, painted pottery, metalworks, and so forth. Essentially, archaeoastronomy investigates cultural astronomy by analyzing the material record. Conversely, ethnoastronomy explores cultural astronomy through ethnographic studies of contemporary or historical societies.

As with any other historical or archaeological data, cultural astronomy aims to provide insights into past societies by understanding their ways of thinking (Criado-Boado 2012). This means that the data and hypotheses advanced by cultural astronomy must be supported by the archaeological, ethnographic, or historical record (García Quintela & González-García 2009; see also Rappenglück 2021).

One of the key problems in cultural astronomy is precisely how we know what the people of the past were thinking about the sky (Rappenglück 2021). Cultural astronomy requires careful, comprehensive analysis of all relevant information. This work must be transdisciplinary, multidisciplinary, and interdisciplinary, depending on the methodologies used (Rappenglück 2021).

Relevant data can be obtained by inspecting material remains from the past and hypothesizing whether they followed the movements of celestial bodies. This involves checking if the arrangement of archaeological remains aligns with the rising or setting of objects such as the sun or the moon, which is the focus of archaeoastronomy.

A single measurement without archaeological or cultural context does not confirm intentional orientation. For instance, a megalith facing north may interest an astronomer, but it might not be significant to an archaeologist.

The way to verify such intentionality is at the roots of the now superseded green archaeoastronomy, mostly based on statistical collection of data, and brown archaeoastronomy, additionally relying on the anthropological aspects (Ruggles 2011). Indeed a key aspect when trying to verify the relevance of astronomy to a given artifact is to consider its cultural context (Ruggles 1999), indicating not only the relevance of the astronomical concept per se, but also any cultural and social implications that might be directly or indirectly connected to it.

In recent decades, significant efforts have been dedicated to acquiring extensive orientation data to ascertain whether monuments – such as tombs, temples, or other cultic areas – within a given society share common orientation patterns. Notable examples include research on megalithic monuments (see Ruggles 1999; Hoskin 2001) and Egyptian temples (Belmonte & Shaltout 2009). This endeavor has been deemed necessary and important to establish that orientations are meaningful data from which valuable insights can be derived.

After the verification of an intentionality, a second step is the identification of a possible astronomical link, if applicable. This could be a difficult task when we lack any written account or possible ethnographic sources to enlighten the data; and even when we have it, as for the classical cultures, it is often difficult to decipher the correct meaning.

While our data may be statistically significant, it is important to note that this does not necessarily imply archaeological significance (Fletcher & Lock 2005: 12). Several authors have indicated that a purely statistical approach may not uncover the meaning behind monument orientation (see Iwaniszewski 2009, or for a recent review on the subject see Ruggles 2011). Alternatives have been suggested, such as the phenomenological approach by Lionel Sims (2007) or the hermeneutic spiral proposed by Michael Rappenglück (2013). Another possibility was presented by A. César González-García (2013) based on a structuralist ladder. Rappenglück (2021) suggests that interpreting data needs a balanced use of diverse methods from both the humanities and natural sciences, considering their unique specifics and circumstances.

As indicated, orientations are crucial data in archaeoastronomy. An orientation is no more than a measurement in space, a direction. Ian Hodder (1982: 132) states that the organization of space according to specific cultural rules can provide information about a society. Christopher Tilley (1996) suggests that places are locations where events happen. In any given social context, the material world, including the built space, is arranged to incorporate symbolic and emotive effects.

In this sense, our studies might provide further data to understand the stratification of the universe in different societies or the construction of mental "maps" with the help of where astronomical events happen (see e.g. Scarre 2002). For instance, Andean communities built such mental maps including both the land and the sky, because "if there were no Sky perhaps there would be no Earth either ... there must be Sky and Earth so that there can be trees, animals, and planting" (Roberta Puca in Cruz et al. 2013).

However, certain directions may have particular significance in temporality. Specific areas of a landscape can hold importance during various periods of the year (Ingold 1993; Bender 1998; Massey 2006). This significance is often accentuated when specific rituals are performed at these locations during those times. Consequently, areas that are spatially significant can also acquire temporal and ritual importance (Gell 1992: 197–205).

Rituals are understood as performances with specific rules (Hodder 1982: 159). These events can contribute to social cohesion by occurring at designated times, allowing for repetitive social actions. The occurrence of rituals at set locations and times suggests that the orientation of buildings where these actions occur needs to align structurally with the activities taking place.

Conversely, time and temporality have helped build a particular site in space; they have built the landscape (Bender 1998). Temporality brings order to space, creating a landscape that includes both natural elements like springs, mountains, and woods, and artificial structures from various societies, interpreted by different cultures (Garcia Quintela & Gonzalez Garcia 2009).

The culturally specific practice of visiting a particular region at a designated time or performing a ritual in the correct location and time helps organize time and space. Additionally, assumptions about the astronomical significance of monument orientations can provide information about time or, more specifically, the concept of temporality in a given society. This is a complex concept. Not all societies may have recognized the apparent flow of time, and those who did might have perceived it in various forms such as cyclic or linear, or other concepts based on ancestral cults or naturalistic cults, among others (Gell 1992: 37–77).

2 How Archaeoastronomy Works: Data Gathering

The usual research in archaeoastronomy involves a series of specific steps, some of which will be explained in detail in this Element. We aim to understand the site and its structures in relation to the surrounding landscape (Prendergast 2015). The three basic quantities we need to determine are the location of the site, the azimuth or angle of the orientation we need to measure with respect to true north, and the angular altitude of the horizon (altitude from now on. For the

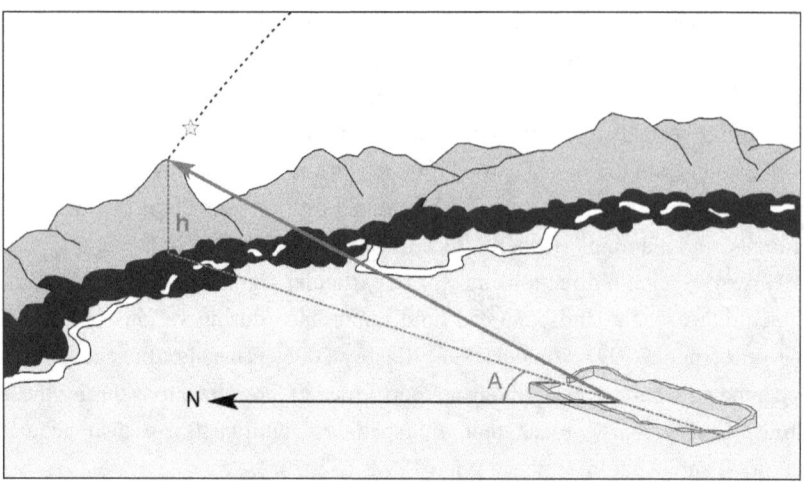

Figure 1 To verify if the orientation of a building is related to the rising or setting of an astronomical body, we must consider the azimuth (A) of the orientation line (dotted line on the same plane as the building), but also the altitude (h, measured as an angle) of the horizon in the line of sight.

rest of the text, we will distinguish between elevation – that is, the height above sea level measured in meters – and altitude as the angular distance from the mathematical zero height horizon of a point in the real horizon as seen from our location; see Figure 1). Every time we extract data from a site or a monument we need to determine these three quantities. We will see later that this is needed to verify if an astronomical event can be visible in that direction.

Apart from our location, latitude, and longitude, we will need to set the direction that we are interested in and measure its azimuth (more on this in a moment). Besides, most of the astronomical events of interest occur on the horizon. Unless we are looking at the sea or on a plain, the horizon will not necessarily be flat, and we will have to measure the height of this horizon, the altitude. In several cases when we are interested in illumination events inside a building, the angular elevation of the window or entrance can be discussed. In any case, such an angle is measured thanks to a clinometer or a theodolite. As we will see, these two measurements, azimuth and altitude, plus the latitude, are the basic ones in order to know which possible astronomical events coincide with the axis of our monument.

The first thing, then, will be to determine the location of our monument. We can achieve this accurately with a portable global positioning system (GPS). If we do not have a handheld GPS, most people have one in their smartphone that

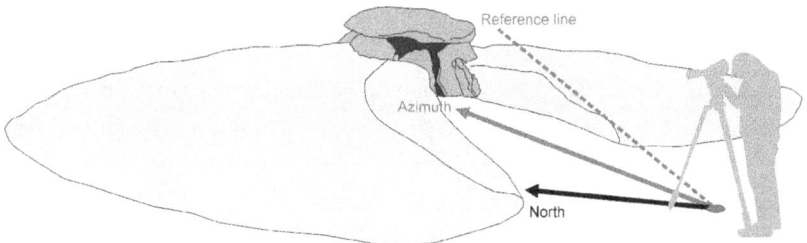

Figure 2 To measure the orientation of this megalithic tomb with a theodolite, we define a reference line (dotted) that is going to be our origin to define angles.

Then, with rods, we define the line of the orientation (Azimuth-line) and measure the angle of this with respect to the reference line. Finally, we need to obtain the angle of the reference line with respect to true north (North-line).

Mind that if we are interested in the orientation from the inside out, in this scheme we are measuring the orientation in the reverse direction, so we need to subtract 180° to obtain the desired orientation.

is ready to be used. We thus obtain the geographical latitude and longitude where the archaeological site is located.

The second quantity that we want to measure is the direction of our interest, so we need to determine that before trying to measure its deviation from north, its azimuth. For example, if we want to measure the orientation of a hypogeum, we must determine the axis of it, perhaps from the inside out, in the direction of its entrance or corridor, if they exist. Once this axis has been defined, we will measure its orientation. This will be the angle formed by such an axis with respect to geographical north.

To measure this angle, we can use a theodolite, an instrument that gives us a very high precision, usually on the order of 1 to 10 arcsec. To obtain the measurement with a theodolite one may proceed in the following way. First, we need to define an arbitrary line that we are going to use as standard for comparison (see Figure 2). Then the line of interest to be measured must be set as indicated before. Such a line can be highlighted on the ground by setting two rods, for example.

The theodolite is positioned at the intersection of the two lines, with the zero-angle aligned to the arbitrary line. Then the theodolite's lens is directed toward the direction we need to measure towards the two rods, and once such is set with our best estimate, we can read the angle between the two lines in the scale.

The next step is to know the correct direction of the reference line with respect to true north. To do that, one option is performing several measurements toward astronomical bodies. For example, with a calibrated watch, we can locate the Sun and record its azimuth and altitude at a specific time. Such readings will be then compared with an astronomical ephemeris for the site.

A cautionary note: Direct observation of the Sun with the lens of the theodolite is never advised without a proper filter. If the theodolite is not equipped with such a filter, we must resort to projecting the image on the surface of a sheet of paper. Selecting the correct projection requires training and practice. It is recommended to test it before fieldwork. The correct projection is that when the whole circle of the Sun is visible in the projection. If the Sun appears with a waning or gibbous shape it is due to the image being cut by the sides of the lens, so we must slightly adjust the directions until the image is round. Once the Sun is correctly projected, we can record the time and read the azimuth and altitude with the theodolite.

To minimize the uncertainty in our determination of the azimuth of the line of reference, it is advisable to do at least three readings of the Sun's position. One can be obtained before doing the actual measurement of the azimuth of the structure we want to measure. A second one can be obtained right after such measurement, and a third after a second measurement of the line of interest. In this way we obtain two measurements of the line we intend to measure and three of the Sun's azimuth at different times.

The next step as indicated before is comparing our readings with the theodolite with the actual ephemeris for the Sun at our location for the times we did our measurements. This can be done in several ways. The traditional way involved estimating the actual ephemeris for our position with the almanacs of the local astronomical observatories. This implied rather elaborate calculations through estimates of the differences in longitude.

However, a much more straightforward procedure today is referring to a planetarium program. One such program is Stellarium (Zotti 2016), which provides precise calculations of the Sun's altitude and azimuth for any geographic location on Earth at any given time. As we will describe this program in detail in Section 10, "Other Ways of Measuring," we refer the reader there for further details. At this point, it is sufficient to state that we are able to establish the coordinates of our observation site as well as the date and time of those observations. Then by selecting the Sun the program will provide the actual coordinates of this body. In this way, we can extract the actual azimuth of the line of reference from the difference between our observations and the value provided by the program.

There are of course other programs that offer similar capabilities such as Cartes du Ciel and StarryNight Pro, and we could refer to online ephemeris providers that give us such data for any location on Earth. One of them is the National Oceanic and Atmospheric Administration (NOAA) calculator: https://gml.noaa.gov/grad/solcalc/index.html.

Here we can enter our location (latitude and longitude, plus the time zone) or set it up in a map. Then we can enter the time of our observation, and we can get the azimuth and altitude of the Sun.

With any of these methods, we must then compare our readings with the theoretical values just obtained. The difference in azimuth will help us in establishing the correct direction with respect to true north of the reference line, and thus also of our measurements of the structure we are interested in.

Using a total station speeds up this process, allowing us to quickly set the correct north direction with its capabilities. Apart from this, the measuring procedure with the total station is rather similar to the one just described, so we will not delve further in describing it.

Another instrument we can use instead of the theodolite or the total station is a professional compass. There are different models and several manufacturers that provide a lower accuracy than the theodolite or the total station, but depending on our objective, it may be enough for our purposes, as we will see in Section 11. One such model includes a tandem instrument with a professional compass for measuring the azimuth and an inclinometer for estimating the altitude of the horizon.

The first element can be used in a similar way as the theodolite, with the advantage that we do not need to define the reference line (or, in other words, the reference line is the direction of the magnetic north for that time and location). This means that we can measure directly the line of interest. To do this, we must set up the compass as steadily as possible. Most of the time we can do this with a handheld measurement; however, in case there is wind or the conditions are cold, we may use a tripod. It is important to note that most tripods contain components made of steel and iron. Since our instrument is a magnetically sensitive device, the use of these elements would affect our readings and introduce spurious results. I therefore strongly advise using either aluminum or plastic components, not only in the tripod structure but also in the screws to secure the magnetic instrument to the head of the tripod.

After positioning the instrument on the designated line for measurement, the reading can be taken as illustrated in Figure 3. This will be our reading for the measurement. Again, this is our raw data that later will need to be processed. Complementary to this reading it is always advisable to take either readings of the positions of the Sun, the Moon, or of local conspicuous landmarks to correct for the magnetic declination (see Figure 4).

It is necessary to add a precautionary statement: For these types of devices, the proposed way of measuring requires both eyes to remain open. In this way we can see the guiding horizonal line of the axis of measurement imposed on top

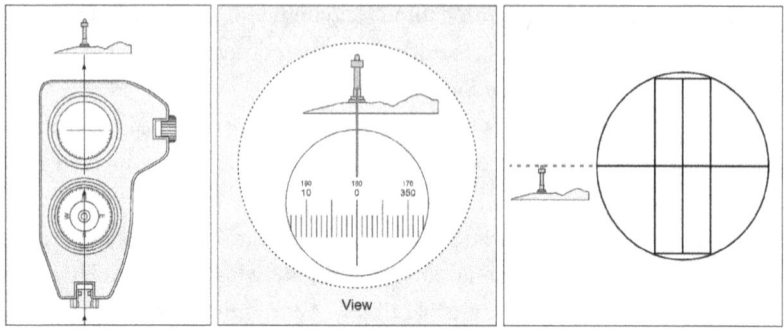

Figure 3 The tandem of compass + clinometer comes with two eye sights, one for the compass and the second for the clinometer. By looking through the eye sight for the compass (center) we need to direct the measuring cord to the item we want to measure to. Then we can read the orientation with respect to magnetic north in the scale. Then we can sight the position of the tandem to the eye sight of the clinometer. Now the level must be placed at the height of the top of the item we need to measure. By reading in the scale, we get the altitude.

of the background image of the landscape in the direction of interest. In most cases, this will facilitate the reading of the direction. However, there is a common problem with this procedure. It assumes that both eyes, the one looking through the lens and the one looking straight to the horizon, will be looking at the infinite (or nearly so). However, human eyes tend to shift when an object is located right in front of one of them. In this way, when we place the compass ocular in front of one eye, the other unconsciously tends to look in that direction. This results in a minor yet sometimes significant alteration of the final reading. This can be off by some degrees in some cases. I would advise any user of these devices to do the following test: Try looking in this way and recording the reading. Then do a second reading with the "free eye" closed, just lifting your head above the compass to verify the direction. If the reading is significantly different (larger than half a degree or so), then we must do all the measurements with our "free eye" closed and using the second method.

The compass gives us the measurement with respect to magnetic north and therefore we will have to correct it to have the measurement with respect to true north. The Earth produces a magnetic field that aligns compasses toward the northern direction. However, the magnetic North Pole does not coincide with the geographic North Pole. In addition, it varies over time in a way that can be accurately modeled (more on this in a moment). On the other hand, the lines of force of the magnetic field are not parallel to each other and, finally, there may be local variations, perhaps due to volcanic rocks or nearby high-voltage lines. All of this can affect our compass measurements.

Let us examine the magnetic readings in more detail. As indicated, we are living on a planet surrounded by a magnetic field; for a given location we can assume a mean value of the magnetic field that will affect our compass readings with a constant deviation from true north. This is a kind of systematic error (see Section 11) that can be easily corrected, as I will explain in a moment. However, other magnetic influences might affect our reading. For instance, if we are wearing metal glasses with steel or iron alloys these are ferromagnetic elements that will slightly affect our readings. Additional factors may arise from wearing or carrying items made of these alloys or positioning ourselves near iron or steel fences or drainage grates. Finally, we must always be away from high-voltage wires, either aerial or underground. Some of these influences we can avoid before doing our reading, and others we can check if they are present by taking several measurements of the line of interest, both along the line in the same direction as the first one (in which case, the readings should be similar and consistent among them to exclude any local magnetic influence), or, if possible, from the other direction, or a perpendicular to it. In these last cases, our readings should be either close to 180° or 90° apart from those we obtained in the first case. If our readings in these checkups change appreciably from the expected reading, we might suspect that there is a strong local magnetic disturbance, and we must then refer to a nonmagnetic instrument.

In any case, if our readings are consistent, these measurements will have to be corrected for magnetic declination, to obtain the correct orientation to the geographical north. As indicated, for such correction we can use additional readings in the field – for example, the readings from astronomical objects, done in a similar way to that described for the theodolite. In this case, however, it is strongly advised to obtain the solar reading either at sunrise or at sunset, when the direct sighting of the Sun is less harmful to our eyes. Otherwise, if possible, we can use the Moon. It is of paramount importance to correctly record the time of these readings. The method would involve comparing our readings with those provided either by a planetarium software or by the aforementioned ephemeris programs. The difference between our readings of the solar and lunar positions and the theoretical ones would provide a handle on the magnetic declination, and therefore on the shift we must apply to our magnetic readings of the measured orientation of our structure.

If these methods are not possible because the Sun is high in the sky, the Moon is absent, or the day is cloudy, we can use local landmarks to estimate the magnetic declination. To do this we must recognize either the top of conspicuous distant peaks or the top of distant buildings such as belltowers, a lighthouse, or an antenna. The ideal would be to identify at least three of these items in different directions of the landscape and take readings of the magnetic azimuth with our compass toward them. Then, once in the lab, we can compare these readings with the ones obtained from detailed topographic maps of the area. We could also use online resources such as the different national or regional geoportals at use, or even programs such as Google Earth or Maps (more on these in Section 10.1). The various readings will surely provide diverse differences when compared to our readings. Then we must take a mean of these differences to obtain our value for the magnetic declination. This is the final difference we must apply to our readings on the orientation measured in the structure of interest.

Finally, another method, in case we are sure the local disturbances are low, is the use of a global magnetic model. These are available at several national geographic information systems online and provide an estimate of the magnetic declination for a given location and date.

One such online site is the website of the NOAA (www.ngdc.noaa.gov/geomag/calculators/magcalc.html). Here we input the location of our site of measurement (latitude and longitude), we choose the appropriate model and date of observation, and we are provided with a value of the magnetic declination, as a deviation angle toward west or east. Remember, this is the angle between the magnetic pole as seen from the location on that date and the geographic North Pole. In this sense, a west magnetic declination indicates that we must subtract the absolute value of the magnetic declination from our readings, while an east magnetic declination indicates that we must add such a value to our readings (Figure 4).

One final method to determine the azimuth of our line of interest is to use a high-precision digital GPS. These devices can be accurate to the centimeter, ensuring precise azimuth in long lines. Such devices may provide coordinates in a projected, meter-based coordinate system like UTM. See Section 10 for details. This approach involves positioning the digital receiver at either end of the line of interest. Then record the coordinates of the two points, and finally with the use of the reverse problem in geodetics, obtain the azimuth of our line. There are several online sites to compute such, as well as python libraries to develop own software (see e.g. https://geodesy.noaa.gov/PC_PROD/Inv_Fwd).

Using either method, we now have the value of the measured azimuth and the means to correct it to true azimuth.

We can consider the zenith as the point that is right above our heads, or the intersection with the heavenly globe of the plumb line. Then the mathematical horizon is defined as the circle that appears when considering all the points that are at 90° from the zenith. An observer located in the middle of the sea and on

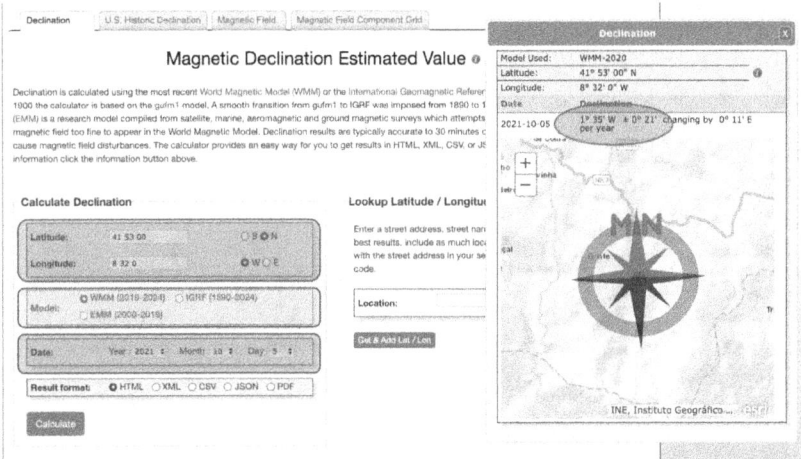

Figure 4 Screenshot from the magnetic declination calculator of the NOAA. After including the latitude and longitude of the site, and the date of the record, a pop-up window appears with the magnetic declination correction needed (oval).

a planet without air could work with just the two quantities described so far (latitude and azimuth), as the horizon they could measure is the mathematical one. However, our planet has a rugged orography and is surrounded by the atmosphere. Due to these two circumstances, we must consider a series of both atmospheric and orographic factors that will affect the precise determination of astronomical altitudes.

The most important is the rugged horizon that occurs as soon as we are in a place whose horizon is not flat in all directions, such as in the middle of the sea. By destroying the symmetry of the mathematical horizon, it breaks double alignments such as solstitial lines. This scales, for small altitudes and intermediate astronomical declinations, with the tangent of latitude. For large altitudes and extreme astronomical declinations, it is convenient to use the general formula (see equation [4]). Logically, an abrupt horizon delays the rises and brings forward the sunsets of all celestial bodies (Figure 5).

Thus the third quantity we need to measure is the altitude of the horizon in the line of interest of our measurement. To obtain such we can use either the angular altitude capabilities of the theodolite, the total station, an inclinometer, or the tandem from our compass-plus-inclinometer set. The reading thus obtained is the altitude with respect to a theoretical flat horizon, and must be corrected from atmospheric disturbances, such as atmospheric refraction, and others, like extinction (see equations [1]–[3] and [7]).

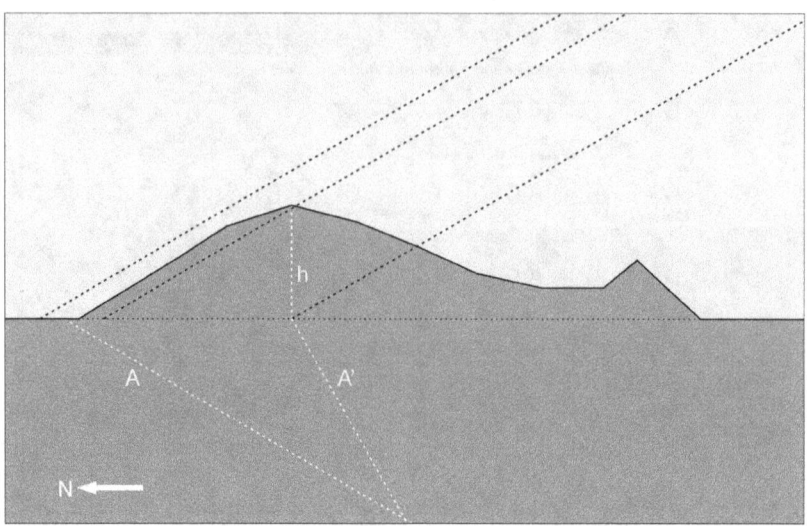

Figure 5 When measuring orientations, we measure the angle with respect to the north (A, A'), the azimuth and the altitude (h). This last step is very important because the presence of a nonzero horizon substantially alters the objects that can be observed in a particular direction. Mind that if the mountain was not present, we could see the rise of the sun at the theoretical horizon, but its presence delays and shifts the actual risings.

The atmosphere has several effects on how we see any of the heavenly objects. The most critical for the altitude is the atmospheric refraction, which changes the altitude where we see the objects in the sky. Atmospheric refraction is due to the curvature of light rays when passing through a nonhomogeneous medium such as the air. It takes a value on the horizon of 34' in altitude, and it is even more below the mathematical horizon, being negligible (for purposes of unaided observation) at altitudes greater than 10°. Its effect scales the change in rise/set times with the tangent of latitude, advancing the rises and delaying the sets.

As a mean with a different density at different altitudes, the atmosphere will produce a refraction angle that is more pronounced at lower angular altitudes on the horizon. Unfortunately, there is no analytical formula for estimating this, and we must resort to semiempirical formulations. One of them is a formula by Bradley Schaefer (1993). The apparent position of the source is raised by an amount R, in degrees,

$$R = 0.01617 \left[\frac{0.372 P}{273 + T} \right] \tan(90 - h) \qquad (1)$$

where P is the atmospheric pressure (in units of millimeters of mercury), T is the air temperature at ground level (in degrees Celsius, assuming a standardized temperature profile), and h is the altitude. Therefore, if we are to use these, we must also record such values at the time of data gathering.

For altitudes close to the horizon, Schaefer proposes an approximation that depends only on the angular altitude of the observed item:

$$R = \frac{0.0167}{\tan\left(h + \frac{7.31}{h+4.4}\right)} \tag{2}$$

One may find alternative formulations in Meeus (1991) or Karttunen et al. (2003).

Finally, our geometrical altitude h' is then simply:

$$h' = h - R \tag{3}$$

A final aspect to consider in general is the depression of the mathematical horizon produced when the observer is in an elevated location. To get an idea of its importance, at 1,000 meters above sea level, the depression takes a value of 1°. The deviation of the azimuth of risings and settings scales with the tangent of the latitude, and its effect consists in advancing the risings and delaying the settings of the celestial bodies. In addition, it increases the theoretical number of stars that rise above the southern horizon and the number of circumpolar stars (outpaced by diminishing their visibility by extinction).

In this way, we measure two angular coordinates, azimuth and altitude. These coordinates are known as horizontal coordinates because the reference plane we take for our measurements is the mathematical horizon. Azimuth is measured with respect to a particular point in the horizon called north. And the angular altitude is measured perpendicular with respect to the theoretically mathematical horizon. Together with the latitude, they are the key measurements we need in archaeoastronomy.

A good practice in the field is always taking a field notebook with you to keep a record of the measurements. There, you may include a sketch of the plan of the site you are taking measurements from, indicating where the measurements were obtained, and any other indication that may be of use when processing the data in the office (like features observed in the field, notes on the local landscape, pictures taken, etcetera).

A final key instrument in the field is a good camera to record as many images of the site as will be useful. Please note that our focus extends beyond the material remains of the site. We are particularly interested in examining the site's relationship with its environment and the surrounding landscape. In this sense, it is good practice to take pictures of the axis we are measuring where we can also see the horizon. It might be wise to take pictures from other possibly interesting directions as well – for example, from the inside out – but it could also be interesting to take pictures from the outside in, or in the perpendicular directions.

Another way of complementing our measurements is by taking panoramic pictures of the horizon (more on this in Section 10.2). In any case, it is always a good practice to make a sketch drawing of the horizon seen in the direction of interest (or of the whole horizon if such is needed) to record the altitudes of several peaks.

In many instances, after we have done our measurements, we may realize that the site has a potential link with the sunrise or sunset, or even a lunar position in the horizon. In several cases, as we will see in Section 11, this includes an uncertainty that we can ascertain. This is why it is always a good practice to revisit the site on the appropriate dates to witness the event, and if possible, to record it. To do this, the best option is planning a photographic session on the site.

First, a note of caution. Mind that while taking pictures to the Sun your eyes might get severely damaged. It is thus advised that you do not look directly to the Sun, even if it is rather low in the sky. Try wearing appropriate polarized sunglasses. This will not save you from the damage if you keep staring at the Sun, but it will minimize it if you only peek occasionally.

The best equipment includes a tripod, a camera (preferably with exchangeable lenses), and a cable release or remote control if available. Photographing the Sun is a bit tricky because we are going to shoot a very bright object, and therefore we are going to miss much of the landscape while doing so.

One possibility to manage the large amount of light is using a red filter, apart from a neutral density one. Filters in general take out part of the light, allowing only certain colors to go through. In this case, as the Sun will be seen reddish close to horizon, it is a good idea to shoot with such a filter, especially for sunsets, when we may start our session when the sun is still high in the sky. The use of the red filter will help achieve sharper edges when photographing the Sun.

Regarding the lens, it will depend on the degree of detail you may need. The Sun has an angular width of nearly half a degree. Then a wide-angle objective will not allow you to verify certain details on the right spot of sunrise, and you may opt for a rather longer focus lens, something like a 70 mm onwards for a 35 mm film equivalent (a short telephoto lens). Indeed, you must experiment on site according to your own requirements.

Then we must find the right camera settings: The best setting is manual mode, or at least semiautomatic mode. First, focus to the infinite and then go back just slightly. If you have some trees or other items on a distant horizon, a good choice would be to see that they appear well outlined and in focus against the background sky. Then try choosing a low sensibility, like 100ISO, or even lower if you can. Aperture at f/8 depending on the lens (for other lenses f/10 may be best) to expand the depth of field. Then you must adjust the shutter speed of your camera. A good idea is to shoot a few pictures before sunrise, or when the Sun is still high in the sky, but remember that exposure time will change during the session as the weather and atmospheric conditions change A modern alternative might be the use of a digital telescope, ready to take digital pictures of astronomical objects, like the Sun. However, the field of view is rather close.

A good idea for recording our session is taking a picture of the whole set once everything is ready, in context, to show where we have done our session and how it looks. To do this any camera (e.g. the camera on a smartphone) will be enough.

When taking measurements and working with them and studying their astronomical implications, it is necessary to have knowledge of positional astronomy, as well as of the movements of the Sun, the Moon, and the stars (Magli 2020). In Section 3, I am going to introduce, briefly, some of this knowledge that is of interest for application in the field.

3 Positional Astronomy

3.1 Coordinate Systems

When we need to define the position of any object in space, we normally use a three-dimensional coordinate system, the Cartesian being the most common one. However, when defining positions on the surface of a sphere we normally use two coordinates, two angles, assuming all points are on the surface of such a sphere (the radius of the sphere thus being the third coordinate). For the objects on the celestial globe, we have the same casuistic: We assume that they are all on the surface of that globe, and we work with two angles to define any position on the globe.

Now, to define these two angles we always need a plane that contains the center of the sphere. The plane divides this sphere in a maximum circumference, and the perpendicular to the plane through the center of the plane intersects the globe in two points, the poles. The two angles are then defined with respect to these elements.

The most obvious plane to use in our case is the horizontal plane of the location we are in. The intersection between the celestial vault (see Figure 6a) and the horizontal plane defines the astronomical theoretical horizon. A line perpendicular to the horizontal plane, the vertical that projects upward from our heads, will define the zenith, the point of the sky located vertically above the observer. Similarly, the nadir will be defined as the point of the celestial sphere located under our feet (hidden by the earth upon which we are standing). The real horizon will only be equal to the mathematical horizontal plane if we are isolated on the high seas with our eyes on the water surface in totally calm weather. On its vertical, the angular height at which a celestial object is located will be measured in degrees from zero (i.e. on top of the mathematical horizon) to 90° (zenith). This is what we have earlier called altitude. And the angle starting from the north toward the point where that vertical intersects the mathematical horizon is the azimuth, measured in degrees in a north-east-south-west direction. This defines the so-called horizontal coordinate system (Figure 6b).

In short intervals of time at an astronomical level, such as a human lifetime, stars practically do not move with respect to each other. For this reason, the ancient Greeks spoke of them as fixed. However, an observation of the sky tells us that they do move throughout the night, due to the rotation of the Earth. One way to see the Earth's own motion is to take a long-exposure photograph of the night sky by pointing the camera to the north (Figure 6a). If we look in this direction, we may see that those stars never rise or set, but they seem to circle around the North Pole. Those stars are known as circumpolar stars.

If we look for a moment at the polar star, we will see that for widely different latitudes, its altitude on the horizon changes, being higher the further north we are. This already tells us that the measurements we have made in the field, the azimuth and altitude, provide correlates to the sky that are valid only for the place where we are observing (this is why we need the latitude, our third measurement; see Figure 7).

Remember, for example, that when we move to high latitudes, the Sun rises or sets further to the north in summer (conversely to the south for southern latitudes), until there is a place where for the summer solstice the Sun does not rise or set; this is the phenomenon of the midnight sun north of the polar circle. Besides, and as we have seen in Section 2, the real horizon is going to be very important in determining which objects might be connected to a given direction.

Thus horizontal coordinates are said to be local coordinates. In addition, the fact that a star rises and sets, like the sun or moon itself, tells us that its azimuth and altitude change throughout the day. However, the "fixed" stars always rise, day after day, from the same place on the horizon following the same path on the sky – that is why we say they are fixed.

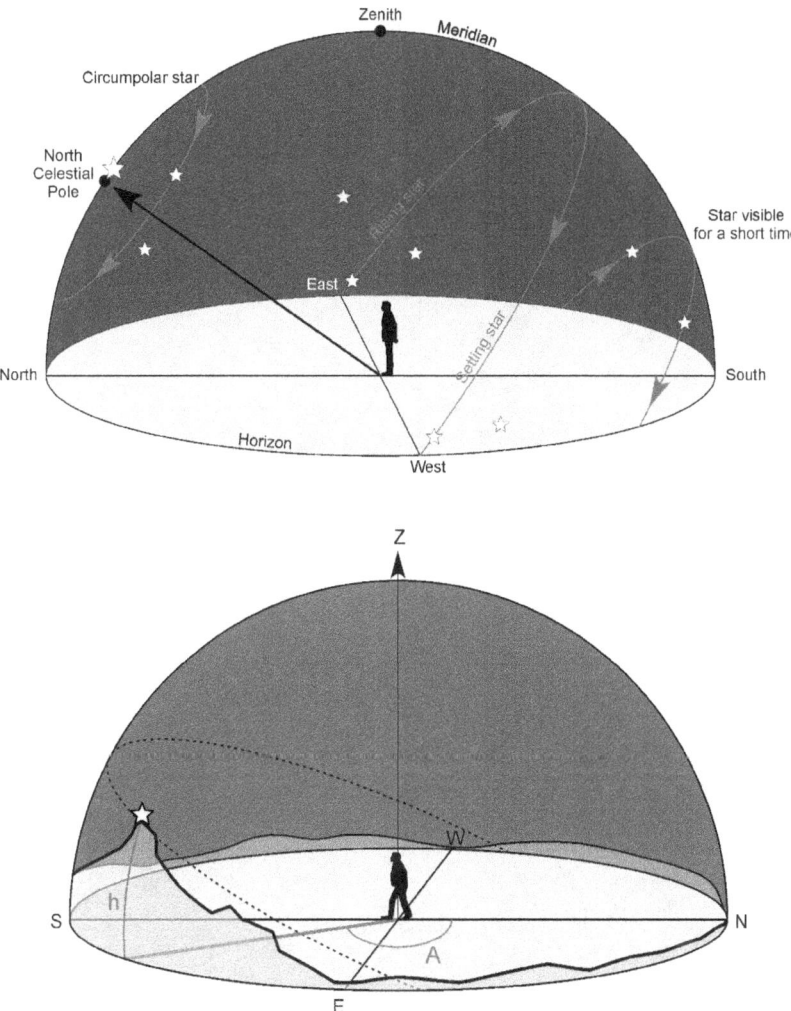

Figure 6 (a) The horizontal system of coordinates is based on the horizontal plane that intersects the sky in the horizon. Perpendicular to it is the plumb line that in the celestial vault intersects at the zenith. The celestial vault is seen moving along the day due to the rotation of the Earth: Stars and other heavenly bodies rise in the eastern horizon and set in the west. There are a number of stars that do not set or rise in the north (for the northern hemisphere) but circle around the pole, these are the circumpolar stars. (b) The horizontal system is based on two coordinates. The azimuth (A) is the angle between the north direction, and that of our interest (the star on top of the mountain in this example), measured on the horizontal plane. The second coordinate is the altitude, the angle measured perpendicular to the horizontal plane, from it until the star, or the top of the mountain.

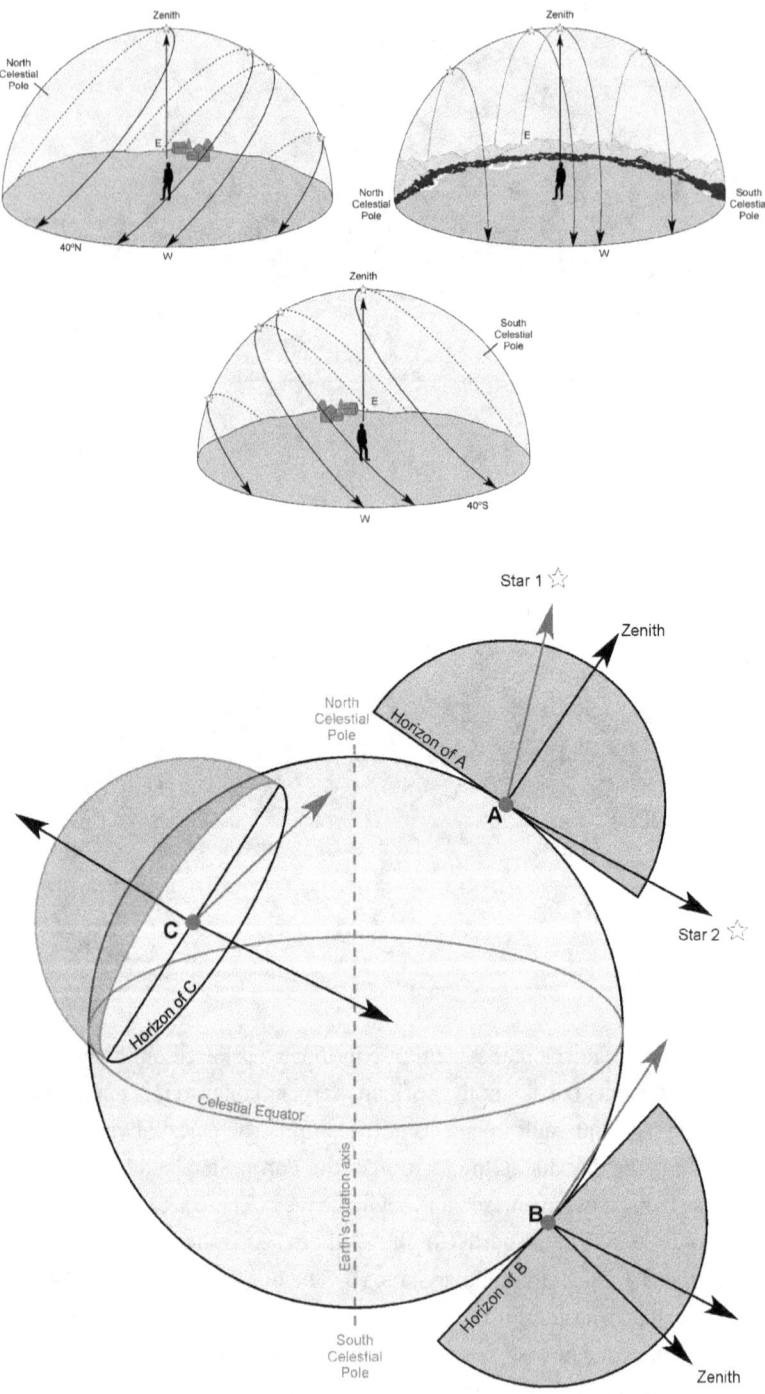

Figure 7 (a) For different locations on Earth, we see the objects always rise in the east and set in the west. However, in the northern hemisphere (top left), objects

That is to say that if we can compensate for the Earth's rotation and the latitude changes, there will be a coordinate system for which that star is truly fixed; its coordinates will remain constant during the day. Also, if we want to compare items from different locations or if we want to know which objects are actually visible for a given horizon profile, we need a coordinate system that is independent of the local conditions.

This coordinate system is defined by projecting the Earth's geographical coordinates into the sky. The prolongation of the Earth's equator defines the reference plane and intersects the celestial vault in the celestial equator. Perpendicular to this is the Earth's axis of rotation, which defines the axis of the world and cuts the celestial sphere at two points called celestial poles or simply the North and South Poles.

Such a coordinate system is called the equatorial system (see Figure 8). Since we are interested in the point on the horizon where a celestial body rises or sets, we are interested in knowing the equatorial coordinate that gives us such an event. This coordinate is the declination (δ). This declination is defined as the angular distance of that body from the celestial equator. Continuing with the analogy of the terrestrial coordinates, the astronomical declination would be the celestial equivalent of latitude.

To an observer of the Northern Hemisphere, as we saw before, the entire sky will appear to orbit around one of those points: the celestial North Pole and the North Star, nowadays called Polaris, the closest star to the North Pole. The circle that passes through the North Pole and the zenith and divides the celestial vault in two halves is called the meridian. This circle cuts the horizon at the north and south cardinal points.

As indicated, the projection of the Earth's equator over the celestial vault is also called the celestial equator (Figure 10). At any time, we will have only half of the celestial equator above the horizon, which will cut the latter at the east and west cardinal points.

Caption for Figure 7 (cont.)

usually have their highest altitude (called culmination) toward the south, while in the southern hemisphere (bottom), objects culminate at the north. Only at the equator (top right) do objects rise and set perpendicular to the horizon. (b) The horizontal plane is a local plane, and each location on the surface of the globe defines its own horizon. The same object (either star 1 or star 2) has different coordinates for each system. To compare the situations at different sites we would need to define a system of coordinates that is independent of the location.

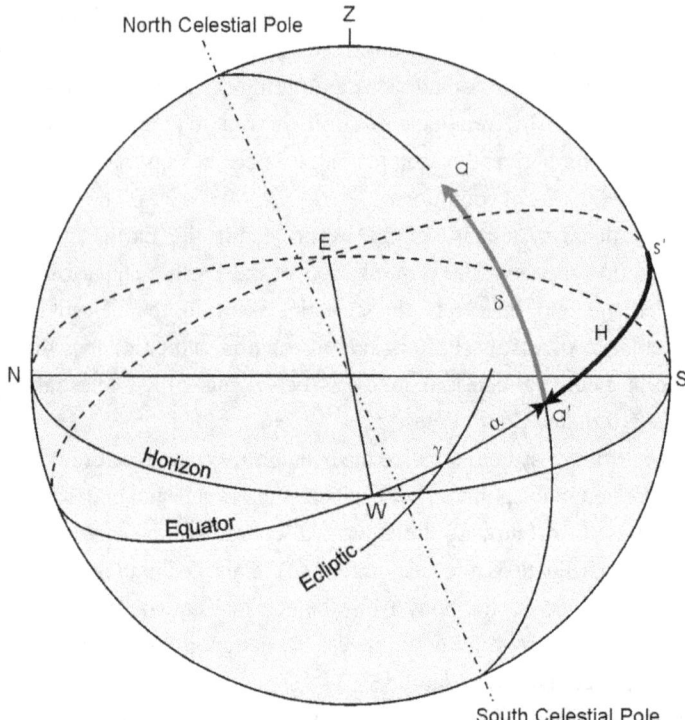

Figure 8 For the equatorial system the basic circle is the celestial equator, the projection on the sky of the terrestrial one. Perpendicular to it is the celestial axis, which crosses the celestial sphere at the celestial North and South Poles. The two equatorial coordinates are the right ascension (α), measured from the vernal point (♈), the intersection of the equator and the ecliptic, and the declination (δ), measured perpendicular to the equator. The circle that passes from the zenith and that contains the two poles is the local meridian and defines an auxiliary coordinate, the hour angle (H), the angle between the line perpendicular to the equator of our interest and the meridian.

The equatorial coordinate system, like geographical longitude and latitude in the case of the Earth, allows us to orient ourselves in the sky since the coordinates are independent of the geographical place of observation and almost independent of time on small time scales. The angles needed to define any position on the celestial globe are the declination (δ), equivalent to the latitude and measured in a similar way to it and ranging from 0° at the equator, to 90° in the North Celestial Pole or –90° in the South Celestial Pole, and the right ascension (α), equivalent to the longitude, measured in hours and which is measured on the celestial equator from the Aries or vernal point (♈).

As mentioned, since this system accounts for the Earth's rotation, declination is the primary measure used to define the position of any given asterism on the

Archaeoastronomy

celestial globe for comparison with the measured orientations. There is a well-known transformation of coordinates to determine declination from horizontal coordinates. This change is obtained from spherical trigonometry relations:

$$\sin \delta = \sin h \sin \varphi + \cos h \cos \varphi \cos A \tag{4}$$

$$\sin h = \sin \delta \sin \varphi + \cos \delta \cos \varphi \cos H \tag{5}$$

where δ is the declination, h is the altitude of the horizon, A is the azimuth, φ the latitude, and H the hour angle (this is the angle formed by the meridian and the circle that passes through the poles and the star we are interested in. Note that this angle changes as the star moves due to the effect of the Earth's rotation).

In this way, using equation (4) we can obtain the declination of an object, since we have measured its azimuth and its altitude and we know the latitude from which we observe. Note that this is possibly the most important equation for archaeoastronomy.

An interesting exercise is, from equation (5), to calculate our latitude. Imagine that by a simple observation, we measure that the pole star for our observation site is at an altitude of 41.76° (let us ignore for now the half-degree distance from the true pole). Since it is the pole star, it is located at the celestial pole, and therefore its δ equals 90°, and finally its azimuth will be 0°, since it is in the north. Introducing all this into equation (5), we obtain that, $\sin(\delta = 90°) = 1$, $\cos(\delta = 90°) = 0$:

$$\sin h = \sin \varphi \tag{6}$$

In other words, the altitude of the North Star is giving us the latitude at which we live, in this case 41.76°. This fact is widely used in offshore navigation to find the position in the middle of the ocean, where we have no other points of reference than those given to us by the sky (and note that in earlier centuries the deviation from the true pole was even higher.).

4 Movements of the Sun

We could have used several other circles to define a new set of coordinates. One of these is the plane of the Earth's orbit around the Sun, or from the observer's point of view, the plane of the Sun's apparent orbit around us. This plane intercepts the celestial sphere in a circumference called the ecliptic (see Figure 10). The Earth's axis of rotation is not perpendicular to this plane but oblique, so that the equator and the ecliptic will form an angle between them called obliquity (ε). Such an angle had a value of 23° 26' in 2000, or in round figures 23.5°. Seasons on Earth are a consequence of this obliquity of the ecliptic, which demonstrates its importance. It is also interesting to note that not only the Sun, but also most of the planets or the Moon will always be in positions close to the ecliptic.

The ecliptic and the equator intersect at two points called equinoxes. For historical reasons, one of them is called the first point of Aries, or the vernal or spring equinox in the Northern Hemisphere, and the other is called the first point of Libra. The Sun rises exactly in the east and sets in the west on days when it is on the equinoxes provided a zero degrees horizon and ignoring atmospheric effects. The point of Aries is the origin of the right ascension coordinate of the equatorial coordinate system just introduced in Section 3.1. The time that elapses between two successive passages of the Sun through the point of Aries defines the tropical year or year of the seasons of 365.2422 days.

The definition of celestial equator and therefore that of the equinoxes requires an observational abstraction and a developed mathematical foundation; we must recognize the path of the Sun against the stars even if we cannot see the stars in daytime due to the glare of the Sun. This is why only under certain conditions can we advocate for an "astronomical equinox" related to the orientation of certain monuments, and why in several cases where we find orientations that could be consistent with this event we might ask what kind of equinox we might be talking about (Ruggles 1997b; González García & Belmonte 2006)

From the path of the Sun on the ecliptic, it can be immediately deduced that the maximum and minimum declinations that the Sun can reach are those of the obliquity of the ecliptic, positive and negative, respectively. When the Sun is at these points, it rises and sets the furthest to the north and south. The Sun is located close to these points for a relatively long period of time – several days – giving the impression that its rising or setting stops at a certain place on the horizon. These points are known as summer or winter solstices (literally in Latin, the sun standing still), respectively (see Figure 9). Since the sun appears for several days in the same area of the sky, the solstices are presented as natural clear markers in the solar cycle (see Figure 9 and Video 1: Solar Range).

Something we can already do is calculate for our site of interest where the sunrise points will be on a flat horizon at the solstices and equinoxes. Again, suppose that we are at latitude 41.9°, since we assume a flat horizon, $h = 0°$, then equation (4) tells us that for the summer solstice, when the sun has maximum declination, $\delta = 23.5°$,

$$\sin(23.5°)/\cos(41.9°) = \cos A$$

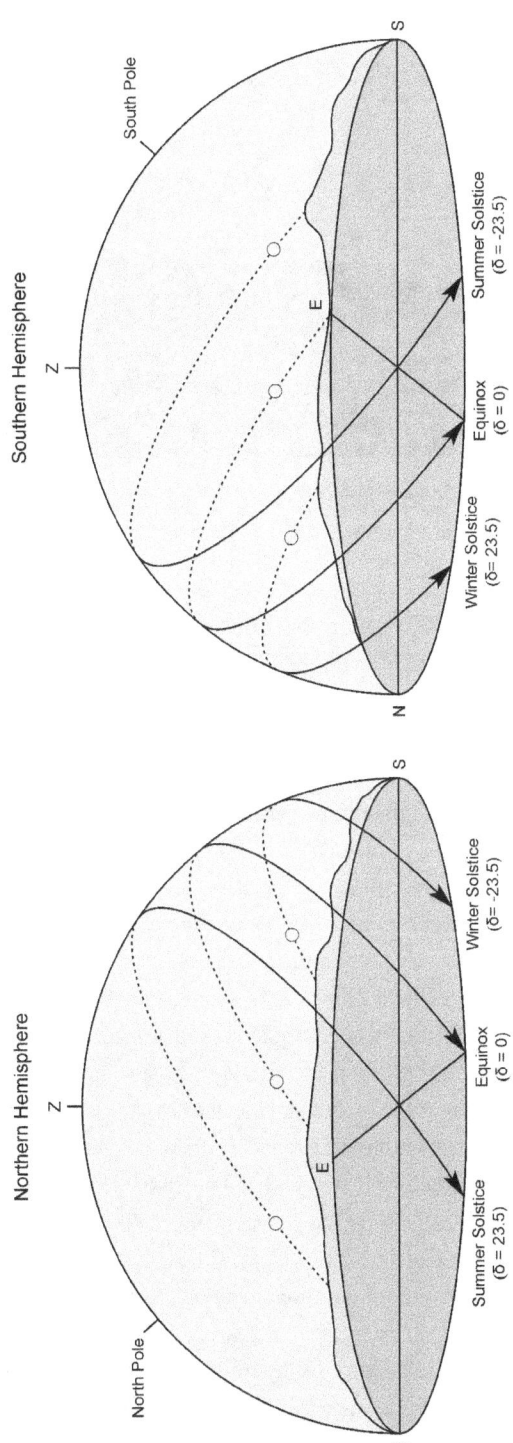

Figure 9 Movements of the Sun in the Northern and Southern Hemispheres. The sun rises always in the eastern horizon, then, in the Northern Hemisphere, it gets its highest altitude, called culmination, due south, in the meridian, while it always sets in the western horizon. The path followed by the Sun is reversed in the Southern Hemisphere, where the sun culminates due north. The northernmost rise and set (declination 23.5°) in the Northern Hemisphere define the longest day, the summer solstice. The southernmost rise (−23.5° declination) and set in this hemisphere define the winter solstice. The rise and set in the equinoxes (declination 0°) will happen due east and west in cases where the horizon altitude is zero, but such an alignment is broken otherwise.

Video 1 The sun as seen at its rise day by day defines an area in the horizon, the solar range, with extremes, the solstices. www.cambridge.org/GonzálezGarcía

from which we obtain that A =57.6°. For the winter solstice, in which $\delta = -23.5°$, we obtain A = 122.4°, and for the equinoxes (remember that for both $\delta = 0°$) A = 90°.

Two websites can be used to translate our measurements into declinations. The first one, done by the author, is https://declination.onrender.com, where the user introduces the azimuth, altitude, and latitude in degrees, and gets the declination, also in degrees. There is also the option to include a CVS file with several lines of these data and retrieve a file with the declination for each line. A second tool, designed by Clive Ruggles, is the website https://web.cliveruggles.com/tools/declination-calculator, where we introduce the latitude, azimuth, and altitude in degrees, minutes, and seconds and get the declination for such readings. The main advantage of these tools is that they include the atmospheric refraction calculations.

We already have the necessary tools to see if the Sun appears at some point in the year on the horizon along the axis of the monument that we have measured. Let us assume that we have measured an azimuth of 130° and a horizon height of 0° for our latitude (41.9°). Putting it into equation (1) we get that $\delta = -28.6°$. This value is more negative than any of those presented by the sun (remember the values will range between −23.5° and 23.5° for our time), so we can already deduce that the sun does not seem to mark the orientation of our monument on the horizon.

If a given orientation lies within the limits of solar rises or sets, there will be two dates when the sun will be at that position. The first the Sun will be while moving northward in the direction of the summer solstice and the second will be while moving southward toward the winter solstice.

Table 1 Solar declination for a year. The columns provide the solar declination for a given day in the year. The dates might be approximate to one day.

Day	°	'	Day	°	'	Day	°	'	Day	°	'
1	−23	8	95	5	51	185	22	56	280	−5	16
5	−22	41	100	7	43	190	22	26	285	−7	10
10	−22	3	105	9	33	195	21	46	290	−9	2
15	−21	14	110	11	19	200	20	57	295	−10	50
20	−20	15	115	13	0	205	20	0	300	−12	34
25	−19	6	120	14	35	210	18	54	305	−14	14
30	−17	49	125	16	5	215	17	40	310	−15	48
35	−16	24	130	17	28	220	16	19	315	−17	15
40	−14	52	135	18	43	225	14	51	320	−18	35
45	−13	13	140	19	51	230	13	18	325	−19	47
50	−11	29	145	20	50	235	11	39	330	−20	50
55	−9	41	150	21	41	240	9	56	335	−21	43
60	−7	49	155	22	22	245	8	8	340	−22	25
65	−5	54	160	22	53	250	6	18	345	−22	57
70	−3	57	165	23	14	255	4	24	350	−23	17
75	−1	59	170	23	25	260	2	29	355	−23	26
80	0	0	175	23	26	265	0	33	360	−23	23
85	1	58	180	23	16	270	−1	24	365	−23	8
90	3	55				275	−3	20			

To estimate the date when this happens, we can use approximate methods. Table 1 allows us to estimate such on the go. So, for example, if we have a declination of 18°, we can see from the table that such would correspond to days with in the ranges (130, 135) and (210, 215) from January 1. These correspond to May 10 or May 15 in the first range, and July 28 or August 3 in the second. A better estimate could be obtained from online ephemeris or software that we will discuss later.

4.1 Stonehenge as a Case Study

A paradigmatic case in archaeoastronomy and in relation to megaliths is that of Stonehenge. The current "cromlech" is the result of a construction process that lasted for more than 1,000 years (Parker-Pearson 2012; Ruggles & Chadburn 2024). Its construction began around the fourth or third millennium BCE as a simple circular enclosure marked by a ditch, with an entrance to the northeast. There was possibly a wooden monument inside, which would later be replaced by those stones now known as bluestones. These stones were brought from a large distance, from the south of Wales. In the last construction process, the Sarsen circle and trilithons were erected, which today are the best-known aspect of Stonehenge.

Apart from the circle of stones, in what seems to be the axis of the monument, and at a distance of a few tens of meters, there are two stones, one lying down ("slaughter stone") and the other still standing ("heel stone").

Stonehenge's alleged association with the heavens is well known. It has even been said that Stonehenge is a prehistoric "observatory" or even a calendrical device (Darvill 2022; but see Magli & Belmonte 2023), but is there any truth in all this?

The first scientific investigation into Stonehenge's orientation and its possible astronomical relationship was due to Sir Norman Lockyer, British Astronomer Royal at the turn of the twentieth century.

Lockyer measured the orientation (azimuth) of Stonehenge, and this turned out to be 49°. The latitude of Stonehenge is 51.18° and the height of the horizon is nearly 0.5°. So, applying equation (1), we have that the declination of the main axis of Stonehenge is $\delta = 24°$ (Ruggles 1997a: 218). This is very close to the declination of the sun on the summer solstice. That is, if we stand inside the monument, looking in the direction of the slaughter and the heel stone, we could see the sunrise on the days around the summer solstice. As we have said before, the sunrise is located for several days in that position. Another interesting implication is that if we stand outside Stonehenge, on the axis of the monument, but now looking inside the monument, from the Avenue, the orientation will now be 49° + 180° = 229°, which gives us $\delta = -24°$, which is also very close to the declination of the Sun on the winter solstice.

As we can see, the value of δ is somewhat different than the one we have introduced for the summer solstice. Is the assumption that the orientation is to the solstice correct? The answer is yes, considering the uncertainties (see Section 11, "Precision versus Accuracy and Error Analysis"), it was in the past. And this is because the inclination of the Earth's orbit, which is the origin of this value of ε, varies very slightly with time in a quasi-regular but known way, so that it ranges from values of 24° and a few minutes to 22° and a few minutes in a period of over 41,000 years.

Today this phenomenon makes the obliquity diminish by 0.46845 arcseconds per year. This is a small quantity, but it may become important when considering large lapses of time. In 4,400 years, the shift would be 32 arcminutes, and therefore in that lapse of time, for the time of construction of the European megaliths or the Egyptian pyramids, the positions of the solstices and the lunar standstills shifted appreciably. Mind that the angular diameter of the Sun and the Moon is close to 0.5°.

This variation is small, but it helps explain the orientation of Stonehenge. In fact, Lockyer used this variation to try to date the monument, obtaining relatively late dates. This was Lockyer's main mistake, as he did not consider the uncertainties just mentioned and the dates that were then given for the monument by archaeologists who discarded his method.

In the 1960s, Gerald Hawkins applied a complicated astronomical model to each one of the possible orientations of the monument. We are not going to go over them all here, since we do not have space to do so (however, we could apply the considerations in the Section 11 to calculate if such orientations are indeed important or if they stem out of pure chance; see e.g. Ruggles 1999 for such a calculation), but these involved not only the sun, but also the moon – whose movements we will see in Section 5 – and the stars. Hawkins wrote a hugely successful book in his time, *Stonehenge Decoded* (Hawkins 1965), where he proposed the idea that Stonehenge was a prehistoric observatory that even allowed the prediction of solar and lunar eclipses.

Nowadays there is a tendency to soften these conclusions a lot (Magli & Belmonte 2023; see Ruggles & Chadburn 2024 for a recent state of the art). Thus any implication tends to be very nuanced. Finally, the concept of observatory only makes sense to be applied in particular cases (Belmonte 2015), to take data that are contrasted in the light of a scientific theory. In antiquity, for example, Ptolemy's fixed instruments (triquetrum, Alexandrine Solar ring, etcetera) were also "fixed" instruments used for astronomical purposes. In "Islamic" astronomy we have observatories in the thirteenth through fifteenth centuries, and in Europe we have them starting in the 1400s. However, in different cultures this concept might not be applicable.

An interesting proposal about this monument (and others around the world) is to study them in relation to their landscape, both archaeological and natural. Close to Stonehenge is the site of Durrington Walls (Figure 10). This is a circular ditch inside which a wooden circle was located. Recent excavations have revealed the existence of another wooden circle inside it and an avenue from Durrington Walls connecting it to the nearby River Avon. This avenue leaves Durrington in a southeastern direction, with an orientation close to the sunrise on the winter solstice (Parker-Pearson 2012). The researchers studying these sites propose to look at the complex globally and interpret them as a ritual ensemble where processions would be carried out starting from Durrington on the morning of the winter solstice, reaching the River Avon, following it until finding the path to Stonehenge, to reach it toward sunset, which would occur in line with this monument. They interpret Durrington as a monument dedicated for the living (in fact, evidence of a village has been found there), while Stonehenge is conceptualized as a monument to the dead.

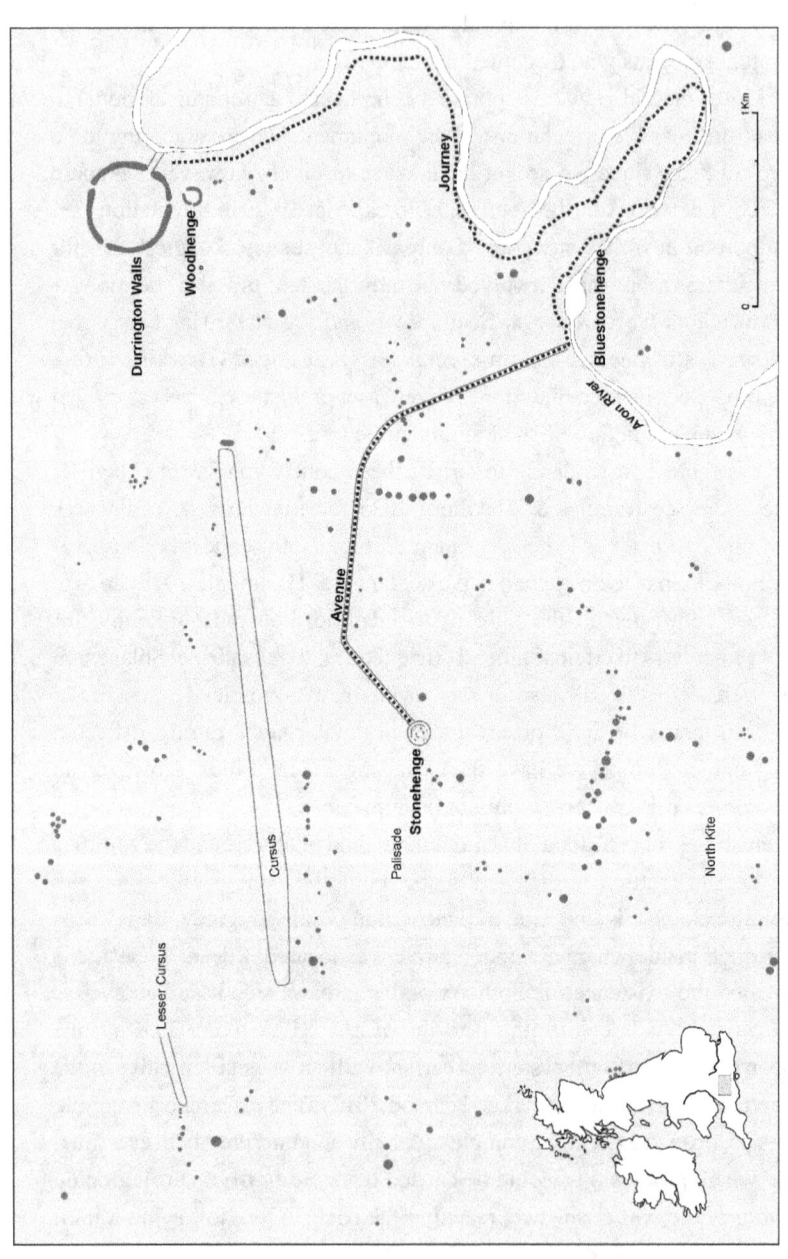

Figure 10 Stonehenge is located on the Salisbury Plain, and its solstitial orientation gets a new and deeper meaning when considered in the context of other monuments in its landscape, such as Durrington Walls, Woodhenge, or the Avenue.

5 Movements of the Moon

The Moon orbits the Earth in just over 27 days (27.321582 days; Green 1985: 173), in what is known as the tropical month. Similarly, if we consider, instead of the same position with respect to the orbit, a position within the stars, we have the sidereal month (27.321661; Green 1985: 173). Interestingly, the fact that the Moon orbits the Earth, and that our planet does the same around the Sun, is the origin of the lunar phases. However, after one sidereal month the phase of the moon is different from the one at its beginning because the Earth has moved in its orbit around the Sun, so the moon must travel a bit further (over 2 days) to reach the same phase as seen from Earth.

At different times of its orbit the position with respect to the Sun changes and therefore the illumination of the Moon. Thus, there are periods of invisibility (new moon), a first visibility (crescent), increase in illumination (waxing), totality (full moon), or decrease in illumination (waning).

The period of the lunar phases is 29.5306 days, which is called the synodic month and is the most widely used lunar cycle. Be aware that this is a mean value: The synodic month varies due to the complex nature of the movements in the relative ellipses of the Moon and the Earth, and there are months with close to 29 days while others have closer to 30 days.

An interesting fact about the phases is the following. Given the positions of the Earth, Sun, and Moon, the first visibility will always be seen in the west, in a close position to the Sun, and just a few minutes after sunset. The full Moon will always happen at the opposite position of the Sun (or nearly so). In this sense, and provided a zero degrees horizon, the full Moon's rise will almost be synchronic with sunset, and conversely the full Moon's setting will happen at sunrise. Finally, the last crescent of the Moon will be seen rising at the eastern horizon a few minutes before sunrise.

To complicate things further, the Moon's orbit is tilted with respect to the Earth's (or in other words, with respect to the ecliptic) at an angle $i = 5.15°$ (Figure 11). Besides, the orbit of the moon oscillates – that is, it is not fixed with respect to the Earth's plane of orbit around the Sun. This oscillation with respect to the ecliptic, similar to the dance of a spinning dish on a surface, takes about 18.6 years.

This movement has a direct effect on how we observe the Moon from the surface of the Earth. Because the orbit of the Moon is very close to the ecliptic (remember, the tilt is just 5.15°), it presents extreme positions like the Sun and rather close to them. This means that the Moon rises and sets on the horizon between extreme positions known as lunar standstills or lunastices. If the tilt were 0° – that is, if the lunar orbit were coplanar with the ecliptic, these extremes would

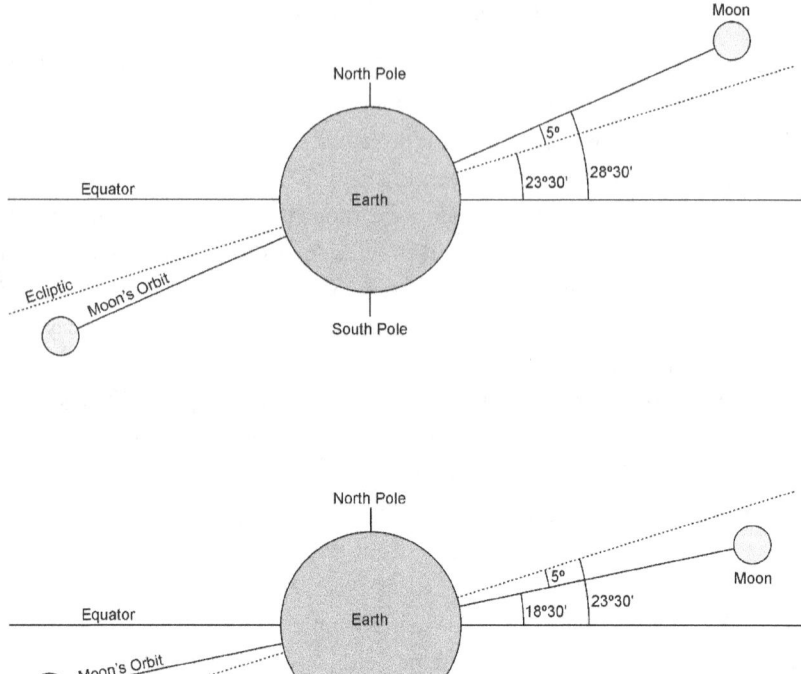

Figure 11 The Moon's orbit is tilted a little more than 5° with respect to that of the Earth (ecliptic), and this inclination (the combined inclination against the equatorial plane) also varies over a period of 18.6 years, resulting in the extreme positions of the Moon changing.

be the same as the solstices. However, given the different angle between the lunar orbit and the ecliptic, these do not coincide with those of the Sun most of the time.

In addition, the orientation of this angle in space changes due to the wobble over those 18.6 years. In this period, the angle between the celestial equator and the orbit of the moon will go from a maximum declination value $|\varepsilon + i|$ (i.e. nearly ±28.5°) to a minimum $|\varepsilon - i|$, (±18.5°) to return to the maximum $|\varepsilon + i|$. In other words, when seen from Earth, although the rising areas coincide for the most part, there will be times when the Moon may rise through different areas of the horizon than the Sun (the same applies for the setting) (Figure 12 and Video 2: Lunar Extremes).

In fact, for monuments where the orientation is outside the solar range but inside the values just indicated for the Moon, a possible explanation would be the rise (or set) of the full Moon in line with the orientation of the dolmen. But at what time would this be?

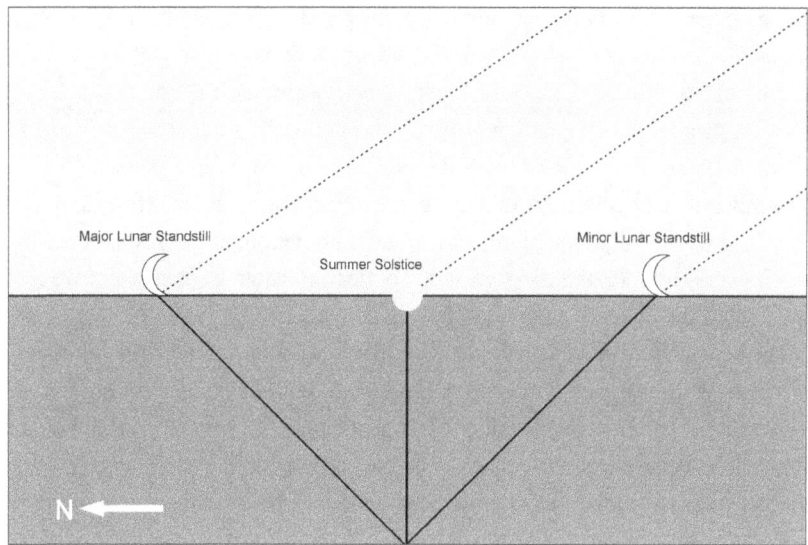

Figure 12 Throughout the 18.6-year cycle, the monthly northernmost rising points of the Moon pass through a maximum (major lunar standstill) and a minimum (minor lunar standstill), to return to the maximum at the end of the cycle.

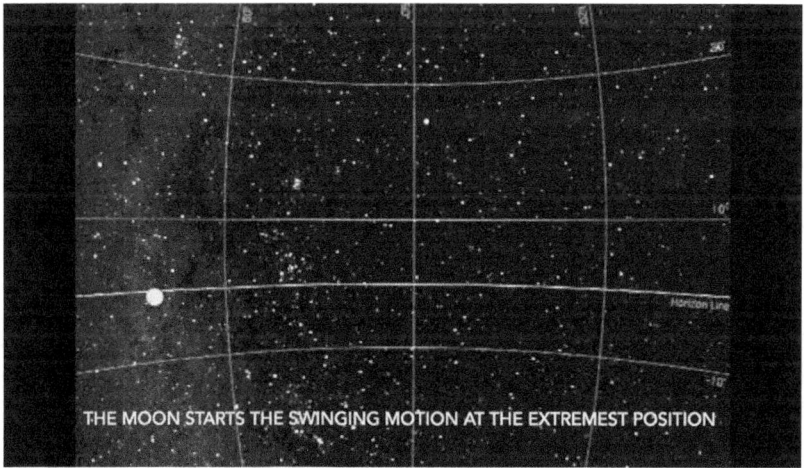

Video 2 The Full Moon at its rise month by month in a 19 years cycle does a swinging motion with two extremes, but these are not completely fixed.
www.cambridge.org/GonzálezGarcía

As indicated, it is easy to see that the full Moon occurs when the Sun and Moon meet in what is called opposition – that is, almost forming a 180° angle in the sky. In this case, if, for example, the Moon rises with an azimuth of 130°, at that moment the Sun sets with approximately $130 + 180 = 310°$, which corresponds to a declination of $\delta = 28.6$. The Sun cannot have this declination, so it will be close to its maximum of $23.5°$, which occurs on the summer solstice. That is – remember the example given in Section 4 – our dolmen could be oriented toward the rising of the full moon close to the summer solstice. Let us remember that at this time of the year the nights are the shortest, and if it coincides with a full moon night, with great illumination, or the low summer full moon, very low in the sky, with its optical illusion of nearness, we can understand the evocative power of such a coincidence.

The Moon has exerted a great influence in many cultures throughout the history of humanity. Remember that almost a third of the planet's population is governed by a calendar based on the visibility of the first lunar crescent to start counting the month. This same event was already used by the Babylonians to begin the months and the year. As we will see in a moment, the Greek polis used a similar system.

Being so close to us, the Moon's distance from the Earth cannot be neglected in astronomical calculations. In this case we say that the Moon presents a parallax, or a parallactic angle. This effect is similar to the one we have for a nearby object and whether we observe it with one eye or the other (Figure 13). In short, the lunar parallax depends a lot on the latitude of the observer and the declination of the Moon at a given instant, so that the greater the difference

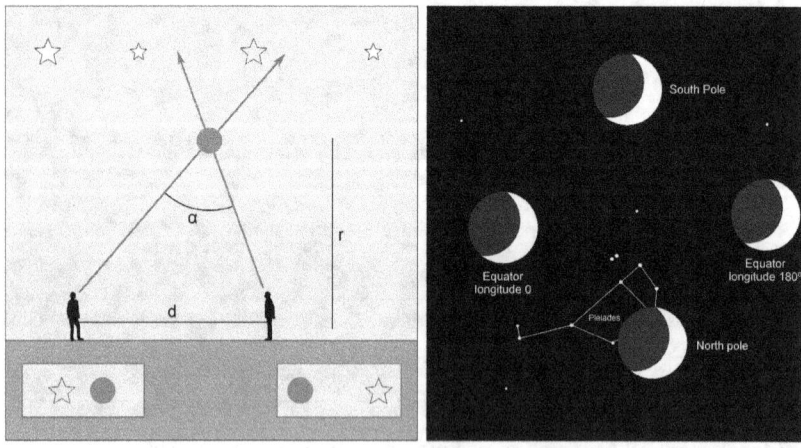

Figure 13 (a) When changing position, two observers do not see a nearby object in the same way with respect to a distant background. By applying similar triangles, knowing the value of the angle α and the distance between observers d, we can calculate the distance to the object r. (b) Effect of parallax on the relative position of the Moon with respect to the stars as seen from different points on the Earth.

between latitude and declination, the greater the parallax (Figure 13 right). By way of illustration, for the Moon in its southern major lunastice, at −28.5° of declination, we will have −50' of parallax arc at a latitude of 35°N and a maximum value for the figure of −55' at a latitude close to 61°N.

5.1 Moon-Facing Megaliths

Not all megalithic monuments are oriented according to the movements of the Sun. A good example are the stone circles of northern Scotland known as recumbent stone circles (RSCs). As the name suggests, these are circles of stones in which one of the stones is lying on one side and flanked by two others very close to the previous one (see Figure 14a). Dated to be of the Chalcolitic period, these RSCs appear in a very specific area of northeast Scotland and show great regularity in their design. The orientation of these monuments has been taken as the line that joins the center of the circle and the center of the recumbent stone. This has been found to be very consistent, almost invariably presenting an orientation in a southwesterly direction (Ruggles 1999).

If we make a histogram of the declination of the orientations of these monuments (Figure 17b), we see that practically all the RSCs have an orientation that cannot be explained by the positions of the Sun on the horizon, but that on the other hand, there is an interesting association of these orientations with the southernmost end that the Moon can reach, its major southern lunastice. This would occur every 18.6 years (over a period of almost 3 years) in which, looking from inside the circle, the full Moon near the summer solstice would set on the recumbent stone. It is interesting to note that on several occasions behind this stone there is a prominent mountain, thus making the alignment of the recumbent stone, the mountain, and the full moon even more suggestive.

5.2 Lunar Distributions

An interesting fact about the Moon in different cultures around the globe is that in several instances the Moon is locked somehow to the solar positions. For instance, the beginning of the year can be equated to the visibility of the first crescent after the summer or winter solstice, or a given festival is due to happen at the full moon that follows the spring equinox.

As we may see, and given the incommensurability problem (see Section 6), such moments will change according to the solar tropical year, and also, we cannot rely on a given fixed position on the horizon to equate the moonrise for one of those moments.

However, it is of note that each of those lunar moments, as we may call them, define a range of orientations in the horizon that may be different from others. For

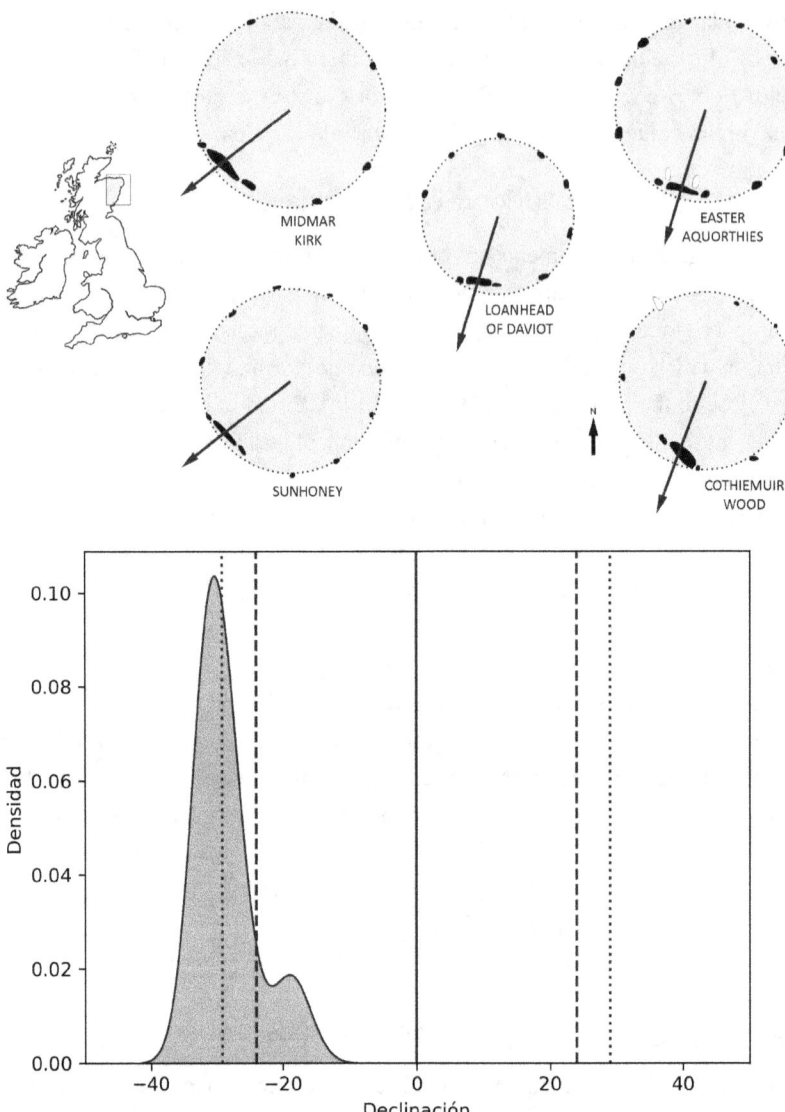

Figure 14 (a) Plan of five recumbent stone circles; note the consistency in the overall design and the orientation of the monument. (b) Histogram of the declinations, the vertical dashed lines indicate the limits of the Sun, and the dotted lines those of the Moon.

example, if we look at the crescents (remember that a crescent will be visible in the western horizon, by definition), then we may look at the declination of the Moon one or two days after conjunction (new Moon), and for a given moment in the year: for example, the first crescent after spring equinox, the second crescent after fall equinox, the first crescent after summer solstice, etcetera.

This is given in Figure 15a. There we can see that each Moon, or if we want, each month, defines a set of declinations. Indeed, in several cases, the distribution of subsequent Moons overlaps for several declinations, but the shapes, as we can see, are different, and we may use such distributions to propose possible explanations for a distribution of orientations that we may observe in our measurements of orientations. Figure 15b provides a similar example for waning moons.

A particular case of these coordinations of lunar and solar movements are the so-called crossovers of the Sun and the Moon (da Silva 2004; Silva & Pimenta 2012). To understand this, we must bear in mind how the Sun and the Moon move with respect to each other. This is especially important with the full Moon.

A full Moon occurs when the Moon is positioned directly opposite to the Sun as viewed from Earth. In this sense, we have a full Moon when the angle between Sun and Moon is nearly 180°. Therefore, if we observe the Sun in winter – for example, at sunset – this means that the Sun is setting close to its southernmost position and we will see the Moon rising in the east, nearly 180° apart. This means that it will rise close to its northernmost position. Along the days, the Sun will set each day further to the north, and therefore the full Moon will rise each month further to the south accordingly. There will be one day, close to the equinox, when the Sun sets to the north of the position where the Moon rises in the east (or in other words, we will see the full Moon rising south of the position where the Sun rose that morning). This was called the lunar crossover by Marciano da Silva (2004) and was proposed as an alternative to the spring full Moon, where we do not need to define an equinox, but just follow the movements of the Sun and the Moon, without the need for a calendar. An extension of this definition was done by Silva and Pimenta (2012).

6 Calendars

Both the Sun and the Moon present a series of regularities that allow us, as we said in the introduction section, to situate ourselves in space. But at the same time, they let us situate ourselves in time. This has been used on numerous occasions since prehistory to build timekeeping devices such as calendars that enable ordering the various rhythms of a society.

The main problem when it comes to making a calendar is that of "incommensurability." In short terms, this means that the tropical solar year of slightly more than 365 days is not divisible by an integer number of synodic lunar months.

The lunar or synodic month is an appropriate unit of time to subdivide the seasonal cycle (the tropical year) into shorter periods, not to mention that the nights of the full Moon must have been very important for people who did not

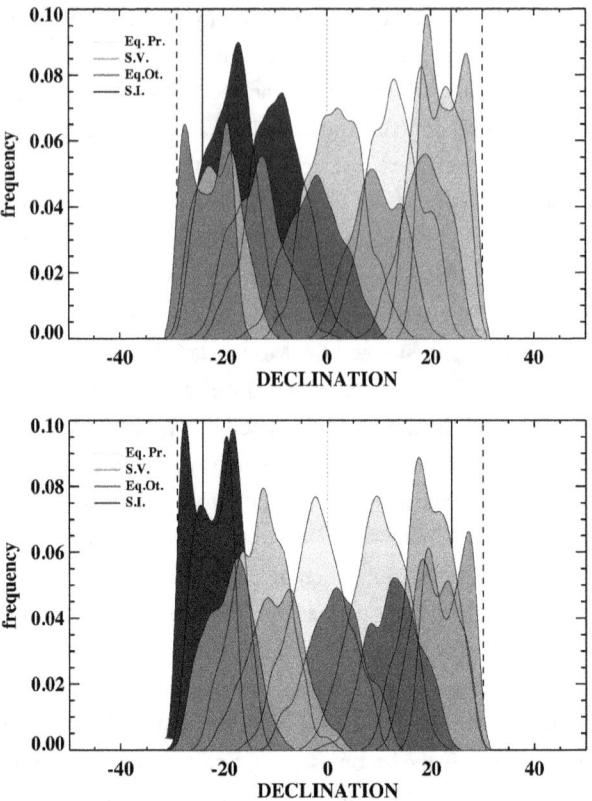

Figure 15 Frequency curvigrams (see Section 11.1 for a definition) for the crescents (top) and waning moons (bottom) that follow particular solar events. Top: The lighter distribution with maximum at nearly 12° is that of the first crescent after spring equinox. Slightly darker shaded double peaked distribution with maxima at 18 and 23° is that of the second crescent after the spring equinox and the double peaked distribution with maxima at 19 and 25° is for the third crescent after spring equinox. The lower distributions are for the crescents that follow the summer solstice (right) or those that follow the autumn equinox (left). The darkest shaded distribution that peaks at −17° is the crescent that follows the winter solstice. Bottom: The darkest distribution to the left is that of the waning moon following the winter solstice. The lightest distribution with maximum at −3° is that of the first waning moon after the spring equinox. The lower distributions are those following the summer solstice (the three distributions to the right), and after the autumn equinox (the three to the left). Mind the double-peaked nature of some of the distribution. This is a typical characteristic of lunar distributions.

have electricity. For this reason, many cultures of the planet have chosen it as the basis of their calendars.

The synodic month has an average duration of 29.5306 days and, as we said earlier, this is a mean value; not all months are equal. Thus the easiest solution is to select alternate months of 29 and 30 days, so that on average we have a month of 29.5 days. This may give us a year of 12 lunar months of 354 days. But what about the 11.25 days that we need in round numbers to complete a tropical year of about 365.25 days? What do we do with them?

Some cultures – few – ignore them, such as Islam. Others, like the ancient Romans, put intercalary months from time to time, using the solstices and equinoxes or the rising and setting of the stars as milestones. Others simply forgot about the real lunar month and ended up developing a unit of the same name that had nothing to do with the phases of the moon – we are an example of this. Finally, there were some whose mathematical knowledge was advanced enough to develop stable cycles of 3, 8, or 19 years, which corrected the incommensurability.

The simplest approximation between the lunar cycle and the solar cycle occurs every three years since 37 synodic months amounts to a total of 1,093 days, which gives us 3 solar years of 364.25 days, 1 day shorter than the real one. Therefore, by adding an intercalary month of 30 days every 3 pure lunar years, a reasonable adjustment of about 30 years of the calendar could be achieved during the typical human life span. However, for longer periods of time, finer adjustments would be needed, so this cycle would result in a "vague" lunisolar calendar that would need periodic reforms and adjustments (see e.g. González-García et al. 2016).

The following approximation occurs approximately every 2,923 days, since 99 synodic months are equivalent to almost 8 tropical years. The difference is an excess of 1.5 days every 8 years, or what is the same, of 1 month every 150 years or so. This cycle is called the Octaetherid and was the basis of the calendar of most Greek cities since its discovery – or rather import – by Cleostratus of Tenedos at the beginning of the fifth century BCE and its improvement by Eudoxus of Cnidus in the middle of the fourth century BCE (see e.g. Hannah 2005).

However, an even better approximation is due to the circumstance that 235 synodic months correspond with astonishing accuracy to 19 tropical years. The difference is only 2 hours and 8 minutes per cycle or, in other words, 1 day every 213 years. This exceptional coincidence is the basis of what is called the Metonic cycle in honor of the Athenian astronomer Meton who supposedly discovered it, along with his colleague Euctemon, in 432 BCE, based on a 235-month cycle of 29.5 days in 19 years of 365.25 days (Hannah 2005; Stern 2012). This cycle means that after those 19 years the same type of lunar phase will occur at the same day in the year.

Despite their mathematical sophistication, all these cycles had a problem: The actual length of the tropical year, as Hipparchus of Nicaea discovered around 150 BCE, was 11 minutes shorter than the 365.25 previously assumed. For this reason, all cycles, no matter how sophisticated, ended up sooner or later out of phase with the seasonal cycle. Interestingly, the natural 19-year tropical cycle of 365.2422 days and 235 synodic months of 29.5306 days is much more accurate than its mathematical approximation, the Metonic cycle.

One final note on chronology that is not so much about calendars: One common problem is assuming that past dates are like the ones we keep today in the Western world. The most broadly used calendar today is the Gregorian calendar, in place with minor modification since 1582 in some countries, mostly the Catholic ones in Europe and their colonies at the time. However, as this was a reform of the calendar under the impulse of the Catholic Church, many Protestant and Eastern Orthodox countries waited much longer to accept the change, and for certain uses (such as religious calculations, like Easter in Orthodox churches) the previous Julian calendar is still in place.

The Gregorian calendar has 365 days in a year and includes an extra day every 4 years (the leap year has 366 days, included as February 29), suppressing only the secular years where the first two digits are not divisible by 4. For example, in the year 1900, 19 is not divisible by 4, thus 1900 was not a leap year; however, in the year 2000, 20 is divisible by four and 2000 was a leap year. This system has a mean year of 365.2425; this is slightly longer than the mean tropical year of 365.2422, a difference of just under 26 seconds.

The Julian calendar was established originally by Julius Caesar in 45 BCE, but was later reformed again by Augustus, after a problem with its implementation, on 8 CE. This calendar, as is commonly known, includes an extra day every four years, to make a mean of 365.25 days. This means that in 128 years we have one day of difference with respect to the tropical year.

As a rule, no matter the calendar and region, when considering orientations toward particular points in the horizon, if we try to convert such into calendar dates, we must take into account the calendar in use at that time and in that place, and its possible displacement with respect to the seasons. This is even more important, for example, in the case of lunar or lunisolar calendars.

7 Eclipses and the Cycles of the Moon

As the Moon orbits the Earth, we may see that at some times it crosses before other heavenly bodies, being planets or stars. These events are called occultations, and they have had a high historical and scientific value in the determination of the lunar orbit, but in most cases, we will ignore most of them for the sake of archaeoastronomy.

A particular case of occultation is that of solar eclipses, the occultation of the Sun by the Moon. It is a great coincidence that the apparent diameter of the Sun (32') and that of the Moon (ranging between 34'6" and 29'20") are rather similar. This indicates that there will be the possibility to witness total solar eclipses, annular ones and partial ones.

In a total eclipse, the Sun is completely obscured by the Moon, or in another words there is an area on the surface of the Earth where the shadow of the Moon is projected. In that area the Sun is completely absent and the heaven appears to be dark as during deep twilight, so the brightest stars and planets are visible during plain day. This lasts for a short period of time, typically a few minutes at most. As the Moon moves rather fast, so does the shadow, defining what is called the "path of totality" over the surface of the Earth. Therefore, the duration depends on where on the path of totality the observer is located. Even if we are located outside the path of totality, we may witness a partial eclipse where the Sun is not completely hidden but takes the shape of a crescent. (In this case, the environmental brightness change is less dramatic by orders of magnitude and may even pass unnoticed when only a small part of the solar disk is obscured.)

Sometimes due to the relative geometry of the movements of the Sun and the Moon, eclipses are not total. If the Moon is in apogee (far from Earth in its elliptical orbit) when its size appears smaller than the size of the Sun, but its path crosses through the sun disk, we may have an annular eclipse. If the path is not crossing through the center of the sun disk, we may have a partial eclipse. In these cases, we could witness how the sunlight diminishes, and we can even feel cold, but the sky is never completely dark, so stars would still be invisible to us.

The problem to forecast eclipses is the relative geometry of the orbits of the Moon and the movement of the Sun in the ecliptic. As we have seen, there is a small but perceptible angle ($i = 5°\ 9'$) between both paths. Were it not for this angle, we should have eclipses every month: Given the relative geometry, each time we have a new Moon we should have a total eclipse. However, due to the existence of this angle we will have at least two (at most five) solar eclipses every year (e.g. 1935), but not all of them will be total. Also, it is complicated to forecast where they will be visible on the surface of the Earth without a proper celestial mechanics theory.

There is another possibility for eclipses, lunar eclipses. Given that the Sun also illuminates the Earth this will project its shadow in space. Therefore, the Moon, when it is in the full phase, may pass through the shadow of the Earth; this is what is called a lunar eclipse. The cone of Earth's shadow is nearly 2.5 times larger than the size of the Moon. This means that if the Moon enters the shadow of the Earth, this lunar eclipse will be observable from nearly all points on Earth in the night hemisphere.

If the Moon enters completely into the Earth's shadow we talk of a total lunar eclipse, but if it only enters partially, we talk of a partial lunar eclipse. Given the size of Earth's shadow, total lunar eclipses can last for nearly two hours in comparison with the few minutes of the total solar eclipse.

Solar and lunar eclipses follow a regularity called the Saros. In a bit more than 18 years (actually, 18 years and 11.3 days) the geometrical eclipse circumstances almost repeat. If today we see a total eclipse in Spain, for example, we know that in a bit more than 18 years from now there will be another total eclipse of the same kind somewhere on the Earth, but not in Spain. The 0.3 days cause the earth's shadow to cross about 8 hours later – that is, about 120° further west. For example, the famous European eclipse from August 11, 1999, was "repeated" on August 21, 2017, over the USA. On each Saros are 70 eclipses, 41 solar and 29 lunar. In short, there are more solar eclipses than lunar, but the former are only visible from particular areas on the surface, while the latter are visible from a whole hemisphere. On average, every spot on the surface of the Earth is expected to witness a solar eclipse every 200–300 years.

It is a rather difficult task to know if an eclipse happened on a given date in the past, especially for prehistoric times. There is an inextricable uncertainty in it due to the irregular rotation of the Earth and the complex nature of the lunar orbit. The orbital configuration of the Sun and the Moon are calculated to be observed from Earth, and thus require a quantity called the Terrestrial Dynamical Time (DT) that runs uniformly. However, the time of observation at a particular spot depends on the rotational state of Earth, which defines local time or its global standard, Universal Time (UT), and its difference is called $\Delta T = DT - UT$.

This difference is measured in seconds and in our time is determined using atomic clocks and astronomical observations. However, its determination for past records is not straightforward, but for several centuries in the past it has been deduced from historical accounts of past eclipses.

The website of the National Aeronautics and Space Administration (NASA) (https://eclipse.gsfc.nasa.gov/eclipse.html) provides the observing conditions for nearly 5,000 lunar and solar eclipses since 2000 BCE to the present and beyond. Be aware that ΔT is drifting freely from circa 720 BCE, so the calculations become less reliable. Note that commonly eclipse type is a global descriptor (partial/total/annular/ ...) while observing conditions name local conditions. The NASA website includes the observing conditions (i.e. the type of eclipse), the location on Earth where is estimated the visibility of the event, as well as the time of the observation. One must be aware of two practical things when using this tool. The first is that while there is no year zero in the Common Era and we pass from 1 BCE to 1 CE, astronomers do include such in their calculations, and this is one case. So, an eclipse of the year −4 should equate with the year 5 BCE.

The second note of caution is regarding the uncertainty due to the ΔT parameter. Without a written account indicating that the eclipse was observed in a particular place, the uncertainty of just a few seconds will imply that the path of totality of a solar eclipse, for example, may shift on the surface of the Earth by several tens of kilometers, perhaps changing the character from total to only partial, or from at least partial to invisible from a given location.

8 The Planets

Among the brightest objects we can see in the sky, we see five objects with the naked eye that all appear to move in the daily motion of the celestial sphere from east to west. Moreover, they change their brightness with time, some of them appreciably. These are the planets: Mercury, Venus, Mars, Jupiter, and Saturn. These planets have been known since ancient times. There are moments when even Uranus could be seen with the naked eye, but its dimness and slow motion with respect to the stars hampered its identification as a planet until 1781.

According to their apparent movements as seen from Earth, they are commonly divided into inferior or interior planets (Mercury and Venus) and superior or exterior planets (Mars, Jupiter, and Saturn). Their relative motion through the constellations as seen from Earth is different.

Mercury and Venus are never far from the Sun (Figure 16a). Both planets can be found either to the east or west of the Sun, so they would be visible either at dusk or dawn depending on where on their orbits they appear as seen from Earth. This has meant that, for certain cultures, the two aspects of these planets, as morning or evening stars, were considered different planets.

The maximum angular displacement of these planets from the Sun is called the maximum elongation. When this displacement is toward east of the Sun, the planet is seen in the western sky in the evening a few minutes after the sunset, setting sometime after the Sun. After the maximum eastern elongation, the planet appears to move in a retrograde motion (i.e. toward west), first slowly and later at a greater speed, approaching the Sun. When the planet is very close to the Sun there is the inferior conjunction: The planet passes between the Sun and the Earth. After some time, the planet is visible again but now in the east, at dawn, a little before sunrise.

In this moment, the planet continues to move in a retrograde motion away from the Sun, until it reaches the maximum western elongation. Then the planet seems to stop for a few days in the same area of the sky among the constellations, to resume its movement, changing direction now toward the Sun, from west to east, in direct motion. The distance from the Sun gets smaller until again it is hidden from sight by the Sun's glare. This is the superior conjunction, after which the planet would be visible again in the west, at dusk. The planet will resume its movement util it reaches again the

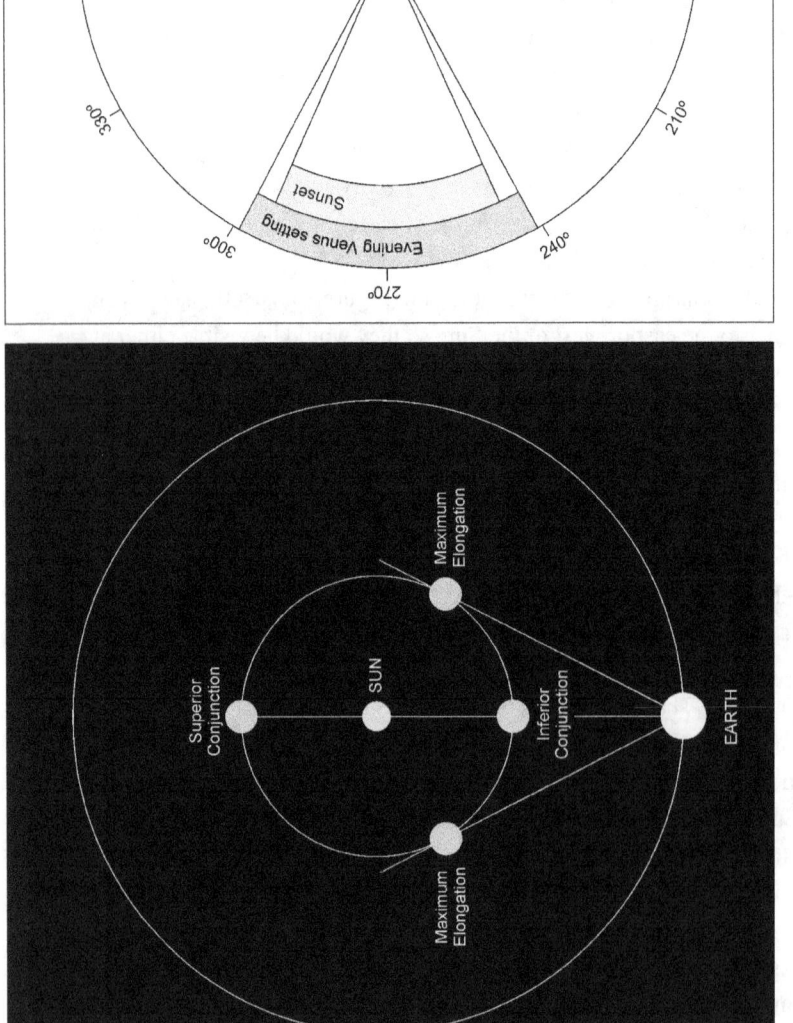

Figure 16 (a) Relative positions of inferior planets with respect to the Sun, Mercury, and Venus, as seen from Earth. (b) Venus circles the Sun in a plane slightly different than the ecliptic, this means that, similar to the Moon, Venus appears with extreme positions further away than those of the Sun (solstices). However, due to the relative positions the morning rise positions are nearly indistinguishable from those of the Sun, while the evening settings could appear different along the Venus periodical apparitions.

maximum eastern elongation. In this way these planets appear to do a swinging motion around the Sun.

A particular way of this movement is that of Venus. Given the relative sizes and times of travel of Earth and Venus, we can see that Venus does five revolutions around the Sun in eight terrestrial years. In other words, the apparent movements of Venus are repeated after these eight years, following cycles of five movements.

Also, it has been noted (see Sprajc 1996) that provided the movements just described, the extreme rising and setting positions of Venus are slightly wider than the solstices. However, Ivan Sprajc noted that these are also different at rise and set: the range of setting positions appearing slightly wider than that at rising due to the relative motions of the three bodies (Figure 16b).

The movements of the superior planets (Mars, Jupiter, and Saturn) are rather different. When one of these planets is seen after sunset in the west horizon, the planet will move day by day through the stars in a direct movement (from west to east), like the Sun. However, its speed is slower than that of the Sun, so this will eventually reach the planet. For a few days, the planet rises and sets with the Sun, thus becoming invisible for those few days. Eventually, the Sun overtakes the planet, which becomes visible again in the east a few moments before sunrise. Then the velocity of its movement gets slower util it stops for a few days in the same area among the stars, to start moving in a retrograde path for a few days, from east to west. After some time, the planet stops again this retrograde motion, to start again a direct movement until the sun overtakes the planet again (Figure 17).

When the planet is in the middle of the retrograde loop, the planet will be in the opposite direction than the Sun in the Sky and the Earth is overtaking the planet, causing the loop or zigzag figure. This planetary position is called opposition. When both the Sun and the planet are together in the sky it is called conjunction.

When the planet is 90° away from the Sun toward east it is called eastern quadrature while toward west it is called western quadrature.

Regarding the orbital periods of the superior planets, it is interesting to note that one revolution of Mars around the Sun is nearly two years of the Earth's, and its retrograde loop is the most conspicuous among those of the superior planets, with an average width of 15°.

Jupiter takes approximately twelve years to complete one orbit around the Sun. As seen from the Earth, it is interesting to note that Jupiter appears to move one zodiacal constellation each year. Or in other words, Jupiter takes one year to move the amount that takes the Sun nearly one month.

Finally, Saturn takes thirty years to circle the Sun. This quantity was often termed as the great year in ancient classical astronomy. These data are summarized in Table 2.

Table 2 Planetary data

Planet	Apparent Magnitude (Max.)	Apparent Magnitude (Min.)	Synodic Period (days)	Sidereal Period (days)
Mercury	−2.6	+5.7	116	88
Venus	−4.9	−3.8	584	225
Mars	−2.9	+1.8	780	687
Jupiter	−2.9	−1.6	399	4,333
Saturn	−0.6	+1.0	378	10,759

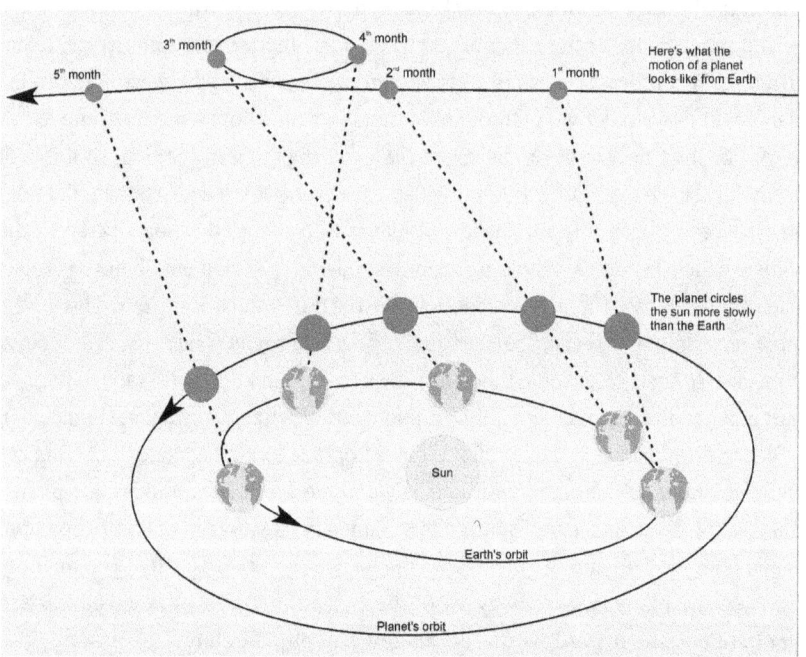

Figure 17 Movement of a superior planet seen from Earth. Such planets appear to perform a loop among the stars in the night sky as their movement is followed night by night.

9 The Stars

The last item we can consider for astronomical orientations are the stars. These have been considered in several archaeoastronomy works because it is known that some stars have been important in past cultures. Some stars appear to be grouped culturally in what we know as asterisms and constellations. The constellations we recognize today are based on the Islamic transmission of ancient Greek and Roman texts where groups of nearby stars are used because they seem to remind the observer of a particular figure: an animal, a hero, or less often an object.

In 1922, in the first General Assembly of the International Astronomical Union (IAU) in Rome, it was agreed that the sky, like the Earth with its nations, was going to be divided into eighty-eight parts, the present-day constellations. In this way, today astronomers know that any part of the sky belongs to a given constellation. This was not the case in the past: Most cultures lived with just a handful of images of constellations in the sky and not all of them recognized constellations the way we do. In fact, several cultures around the globe, even today, recognize the so-called dark constellations formed by the shapes of the dark clouds in the Milky Way.

Finally, apart from the stars, the Milky Way itself could be related sometimes with particular directions. In this sense, when this is the case, we must calculate the visibility of this elusive nebulous path on the sky.

One thing everyone notices while looking at the starry sky is that not all stars appear with the same brightness. Due to their size and distance, some stars appear brighter than others, and this is very important as the brightest stars are usually the ones that appear more prominently in oral and written records and therefore are the ones we would consider first when relating to orientations.

One important exception to this is a cluster or group of relatively dim young stars known in the West as the Pleiades. These stars, of relatively low brightness, appear prominently in most cultures on Earth due to their grouped nature that makes them conspicuous to naked eye and due to being close to the ecliptic, appearing thus often close to the Sun, but also to the Moon and the planets.

The brightness of the stars (and planets) is measured in magnitudes. This is a concept Hipparchus introduced already in the second century BCE when he defined the brightest stars as being of first magnitude and the dimmest as being of sixth magnitude. The system is basically the same today, although today we consider some stars to be brighter than first magnitude (Sirius for instance is the brightest star in the sky and has a magnitude of -1.46; see Table 3 for the values of the brightest stars) and astronomers extend this scale to negative values and beyond sixth magnitude for those that are observable only through binoculars or a telescope.

As noted, the light coming from the stars is dampened by the Earth's atmosphere, causing what is called atmospheric extinction. It depends a lot on the weather conditions and can be extreme in case of haze or fog. Its effect is especially important near the horizon as the layer of air that the light must pass through is much greater. In fact, it is common that most stars and even, depending on weather conditions, the planets or the Moon are not seen at the horizon.

Table 3 Gives the declination for the brightest stars at different epochs. The columns provide the star's name, its magnitude (the smaller the magnitude the brighter the star), and the declination for each year indicated at the top.

Star	mag	-3000	-2500	-2000	-1500	-1000	-500	1	500	1000	1500	2000
Sirius	-1.46	-22°20'	-20°41'	-19°16'	-18°3'	-17°5'	-16°22'	-15°55'	-15°43'	-15°47'	-16°7'	-16°43'
Canopus	-0.72	-56°20'	-55°25'	-54°37'	-53°56'	-53°22'	-52°55'	-52°37'	-52°26'	-52°23'	-52°28'	-52°42'
Arcturus	-0.04	48°55'	46°1'	43°1'	39°56'	36°49'	33°43'	30°38'	27°37'	24°41'	21°52'	19°11'
α Cen	-0.01	-39°1'	-41°11'	-43°29'	-45°41'	-48°0'	-50°19'	-52°37'	-54°51'	-57°0'	-59°51'	-60°50'
Vega	0.03	43°55'	42°32'	41°19'	40°19'	39°29'	38°52'	38°26'	38°13'	38°12'	38°23'	38°47'
Capella	0.08	25°54'	28°41'	31°24'	34°2'	36°32'	38°51'	40°56'	42°45'	44°13'	45°19'	46°0'
Rigel	0.12	-25°47'	-23°11'	-20°43'	-18°24'	-16°15'	-14°19'	-12°35'	-11°6'	-9°51'	-8°53'	-8°12'
Procyon	0.38	3°9'	4°33'	5°51'	6°52'	7°35'	7°59'	8°4'	7°49'	7°16'	6°23'	5°13'
Achernar	0.46	-82°37'	-81°5'	-78°51'	-76°17'	-73°33'	-70°46'	-67°57'	-65°11'	-62°27'	-59°48'	-57°14'
Betelgeuse	0.5	-7°35'	-5°31'	-2°42'	-0°32'	1°25'	3°8'	4°36'	5°43'	6°38'	7°11'	7°24'
β Cen	0.61	-33°43'	-36°10'	-38°44'	-41°23'	-44°7'	-46°54'	-49°43'	-52°30'	-55°15'	-57°53'	-60°22'
Altair	0.77	9°54'	8°29'	7°21'	6°30'	5°56'	5°41'	5°43'	6°4'	6°43'	7°39'	8°52'
Aldebaran	0.85	-5°1'	-2°14'	0°30'	3°9'	5°41'	8°3'	10°15'	12°13'	13°56'	15°23'	16°30'
Antares	0.96	-3°54'	-6°42'	-9°30'	-12°14'	-14°52'	-17°21'	-19°40'	-21°46'	-23°37'	-25°11'	-26°25'
Spica	0.98	1°54'	12°54'	10°31'	8°0'	5°21'	2°36'	-0°11'	-2°59'	-5°46'	-8°30'	-11°9'
Pollux	1.14	22°49'	24°48'	26°32'	27°58'	29°4'	29°49'	30°13'	30°13'	29°51'	29°7'	28°1'
Fomalhaut	1.16	-44°12'	-44°23'	-44°8'	-43°26'	-42°20'	-40°52'	-39°4'	-37°0'	-34°42'	-32°13'	-29°37'
Deneb	1.25	36°15'	36°16'	36°29'	36°55'	37°33'	38°22'	39°24'	40°36'	42°0'	43°33'	45°17'
β Crux	1.25	-33°59'	-36°5'	-38°22'	-40°46'	-43°17'	-45°54'	-48°36'	-51°21'	-54°9'	-56°56'	-59°41'
α Crux	1.33	-37°55'	-39°56'	-42°7'	-44°27'	-46°53'	-49°26'	-52°5'	-54°47'	-57°33'	-60°19'	-63°6'
Regulus	1.35	23°49'	24°7'	24°2'	23°36'	22°48'	21°40'	20°14'	18°30'	16°32'	14°20'	11°58'
Alkaid	1.85	75°45'	73°33'	71°3'	68°22'	65°36'	62°47'	59°58'	57°12'	54°29'	51°51'	49°18'
Alioth	1.75	77°52'	77°33'	76°23'	74°32'	72°15'	69°43'	67°1'	64°15'	61°28'	58°41'	55°57'
Dubhe	2	69°0'	70°55'	72°18'	73°3'	73°3'	72°20'	70°57'	69°5'	66°51'	64°22'	61°44'
Polaris	1.95	62°32'	65°0'	67°31'	70°7'	72°46'	75°29'	78°13'	80°59'	83°47'	86°35'	89°16'
Alcyone	2.87	-0°24'	2°24'	5°13'	8°1'	10°46'	13°26'	15°58'	18°20'	20°30'	22°27'	24°6'
Thuban	3.65	88°46'	88°22'	85°33'	82°45'	79°59'	77°14'	74°32'	71°54'	69°19'	66°48'	66°21'

Thus, depending on the altitude, the light from the object crosses a larger amount of atmosphere close to the horizon than toward the zenith. This will scatter the light, dimming the visibility of the objects. This can be calculated by the extinction coefficient (k) that depends on the air mass and the wavelength. For visual wavelengths can be approximated by

$$k = 0.2 \; e^{-\left(\frac{H}{8.2}\right)} \tag{7}$$

where H is the observer's height in kilometers above sea level; k is measured in magnitudes per air mass (Flanders & Creed 2008).

As a rule of thumb, to be visible a star must be at least as high in degrees above the mathematical horizon for each stellar magnitude it has. For example, with this rule Vega (zero magnitude) will be visible from the very moment of its rise but the Pleiades, whose brightest star is of third magnitude, will not be visible until it is at least at 3° of altitude. This effect delays the visual appearance and brings forward the disappearing of the stars.

The stars, as we indicated earlier, behave as "fixed stars" for short elapses of time, like a human lifetime – that is, they have a nearly constant declination, and therefore, for a particular observing location, they rise and set at the same azimuths each night. Earlier we defined periods of time with respect to the Sun – these are the tropical year – and equivalently we may have the solar day.

Similarly, we can use the stars as references to define periods of time; these are the sideral day and the sidereal year. The sideral day is the time of a revolution of the Earth with respect to the stars and is 23 hours and 56 minutes; it takes 4 minutes longer for the sun to be in the meridian, so the solar day is 24 hours long (Figure 18).

As we saw before, due to the movement of the Sun through the sky as seen from Earth, its rising and settings appear to move along the horizon. However, due to the difference in time between the solar and sideral days, we see the Sun moving along the constellations through the ecliptic. In fact, the ecliptic crosses a number of constellations, those commonly known as the Zodiac or the zodiacal constellations. When making such movement, the stars positioned behind or near the Sun are not visible due to its brightness. In a few days, stars currently hidden by the Sun will reappear, while others now visible will move behind it caused by that 4-minute difference.

This movement has a consequence: There are important relative positions of a star with respect to the Sun. Depending on the distance from the Sun of those stars and their brightness, the amount of time they will be "invisible" is variable. Then, the first important moment would be the first time a star (or group of stars: asterism) is visible again rising in the morning a few minutes before sunrise,

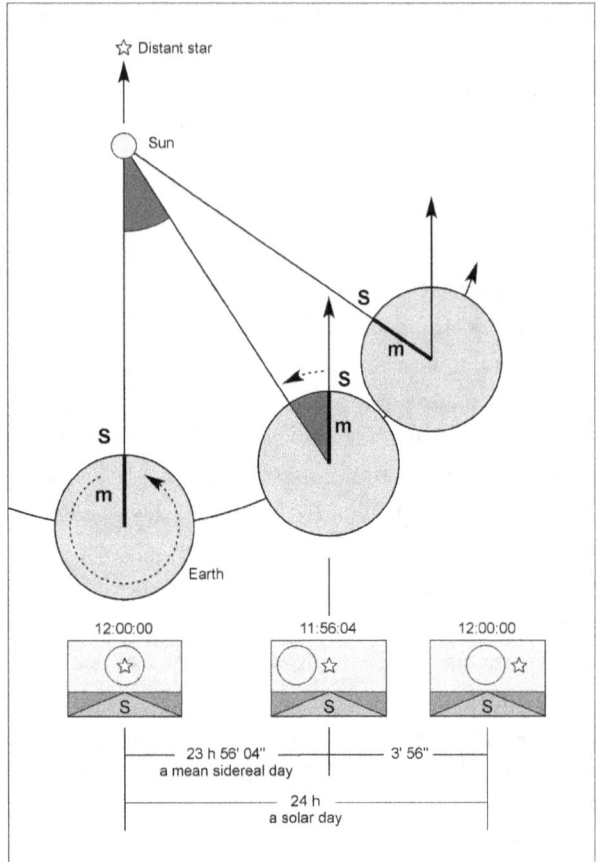

Figure 18 Differences in the definition of a day depend on whether we use the Sun or the Stars as a reference. The difference arises due to the translational movement of the Earth around the Sun.

after its period of invisibility. This is commonly called the heliacal rising (Figure 19).

Another important moment would be when the star, whose setting was still visible in the evening right after sunset, disappears behind the Sun. This is the so-called heliacal setting.

There are another two important relative positions between the stars and the Sun. Given the 4 minutes of difference, each day the stars that we saw rising slightly earlier than the Sun would rise each night slightly earlier, until there is the day when they rise somewhat after the Sun sets. This is the last time this rising of those stars would be directly visible, because a few days later this rising would happen when the Sun is still above the horizon, therefore blinding all visibility of the stars. That event is called the acronychal rising of the star.

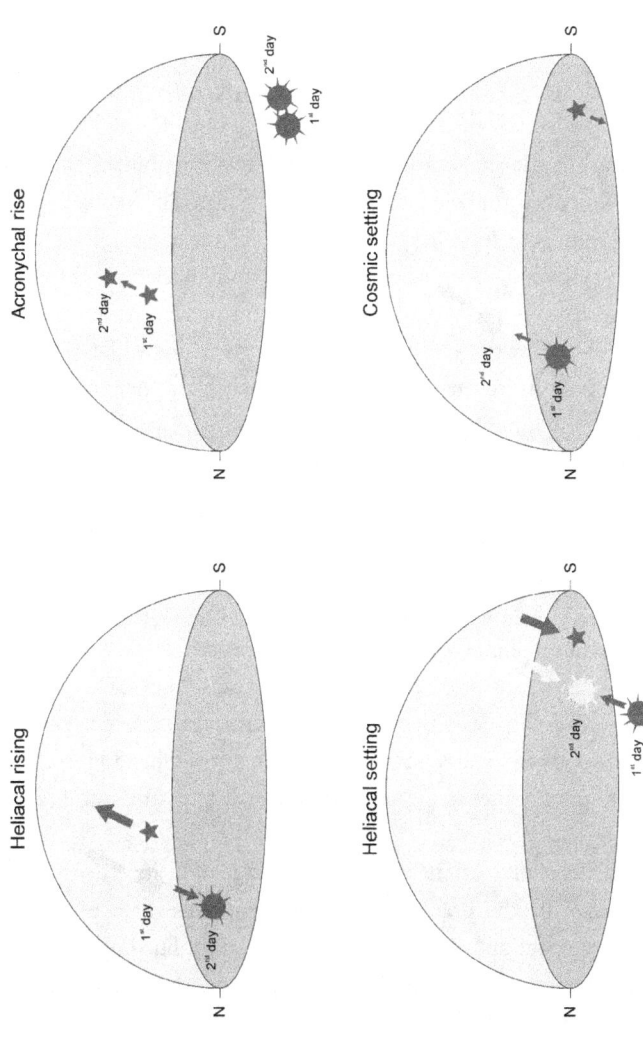

Figure 19 The relative positions of the stars and the Sun change nigh: by night, so we will be able to define several important positions. In the heliacal rising, the first day we have the star in conjunction with the Sun, while in the second day the star is seen rising a few minutes before sunrise. In the heliacal setting, on day one we see the setting of the star right after sunset, while on the following day we do not see such star setting as it happens before or with the sunset. For the acronychal rise, we see the rising of the star right after sunset. Finally, for the cosmic setting, we have the last day when we see the setting of a star right before sunrise.

The setting of the star might still be visible because it happens during the night; however, the same movement affects the setting, and there will be a fourth important relative moment. This is the last time the setting of the star is seen before the sun rises. This is called the cosmic setting of the star.

Note that the terminology in the literature is often inverted. The word *acronychal* often refers to nightfall, while *heliacal* refers to morning, but others (like here) explain heliacal setting in the evening.

Do not panic; a number of astronomical softwares are available to compute the relative positions and these important moments for different positions on Earth.

One first such software is the Planetary, Lunar and Stellar Visibilitys software, which can be downloaded for free from www.alcyone.de. This software, running only under Windows, offers the possibility to calculate the relevant stellar positions, for several hundreds of stars, on any location on Earth and for several centuries in the past. An alternative is the open-source planetarium software Stellarium. This software, which we will describe in more detail in Section 10.2, includes a plug-in for the observability of the stellar phenomena. By selecting the star, and clicking on the "observability" option, we will have the calculation ready to use for the time and location of our choice.

Another possibility to consider is the conjunction of some stars with the Moon at particular phases. The revolution of the Moon with respect to the stars (sidereal month) amounts to 27.312 days. This means that in a bit more than 27 days the Moon appears in a similar area of the sky with respect to the stars; however, the synodic month, the one following the lunar phases, as we saw, is on average 29.53 days. This is a difference of slightly more than 2 days. Despite these, some calendars, like the Babylonian one, appeared to consider the conjunction of the full Moon of Nissan and the Pleiades to know when to insert an intercalary month, thus introducing a rather complicated structure into the calendar.

The basic problem with stellar orientations or with stellar visibility from a given location is known as the precession of the equinoxes. Due to the gravitational effects of the Sun and the Moon, plus secondary but important effects of the rest of the planets, the Earth makes a precessional movement like that of a spinning top (Figure 20 and Video 3: Precession). The Earth thus revolves around its axis, and this axis in turn describes another turn. This is called precession.

The basic effect of this spinning motion is that the intersection points between the celestial equator and the ecliptic change over time. That is, the positions of the vernal and autumnal equinoxes change with respect to the stars. A clear effect of this is the change of the declination of the stars (see Table 3). In

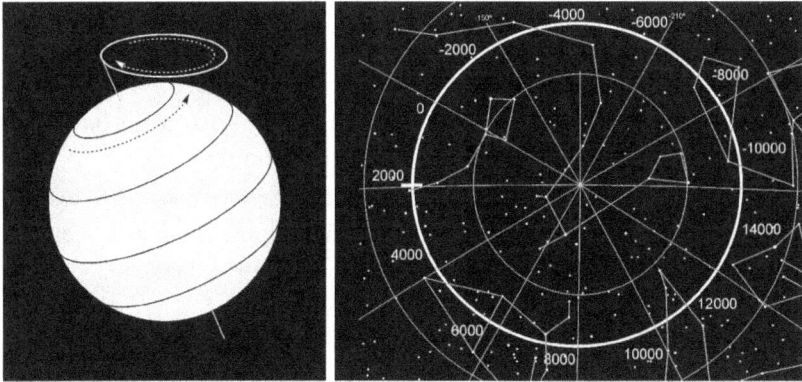

Figure 20 The precession of the equinoxes is due to the precessional movement of the Earth's rotation axis. As a consequence, this axis, and therefore the celestial poles, change in direction among the stars, so the poles change their positions with respect to the stars.

Video 3 The Earth's axis, as that of a spinning wheel, presents a precessional motion with a cycle of nearly 26000 years. This has a direct influence how we see the stars. www.cambridge.org/GonzálezGarcía

consequence, the stars visible from a particular location at a certain epoch change. The relative positions of the stars – that is, the position of one star with respect to the rest – do not change because of this. But from a particular location, stars that are visible at a given time might become invisible at another.

Be aware that this does not affect where we see the sun rising or setting at the time of the equinoxes or the solstices, or along the year, but which constellations are behind it at that moment. This means that the precession of the equinoxes has no effect on the positions of the Sun at the solstices, which instead is affected, as we saw, by the variation of the obliquity of the ecliptic.

In short, the two movements are different: While the variation of the obliquity is a change in this angle of the Earth's axis from a maximum and minimum values over 41,000 years, the precessional movement is a spinning motion of such axis with a timing of one revolution in 25,776 years.

Consequently, because of precession, stars decrease their ecliptic longitude at a rate of 50.2564 arcminutes per year, which leads to a variation of 30° in about 2,150 years.

From the perspective of an observer, there are a number of fundamental consequences. The most obvious is the secular variation of the position of the celestial pole, which describes a circle around the pole of the ecliptic every 25,776 years. Consequently, Polaris has been the closest bright star to the pole for only approximately 1,500 years. For the time of Columbus, the difference was about 5°. At the change of eras, Kochab was the polar star, and 15,000 years ago, during the Palaeolithic, it was Vega (Figure 20).

The precession of the equinoxes also moves the equinox on the ecliptic, resulting in the variation of the right ascension but also the declination of the stars. This implies changes to their rising and setting positions. In astrology, those born around March 21 are said to be Aries. This is because in the time of Ptolemy (second century CE) the equinox occurred in this constellation. However, in a few decades from now the equinox will occur in the constellation Aquarius. The rhythm of the equinox movement is one revolution in 25,776 years. Finally, another consequence is that the rising and setting positions of the constellations change over time, causing some constellations to cease to be visible from some places, while others become so.

As a consequence, we observe the shift of the dates of the heliacal rises and sets of the stars over time due to variations in declination and right ascension. This means that, when calculating the heliacal rising or the other stellar positions, we must also consider the precession of the equinoxes and take the time difference into careful consideration.

Finally, due to the differential rotation of the galaxy that drags the Sun and the other stars, these present what is called their proper motion. This is very small and, in most cases, negligible for our interests, although in few cases and for very long times in the past this might be taken into account.

A particular case of possible stellar orientation that I would like to mention is that of the pyramids of Egypt (Figure 21). These megaliths, of which we count more than

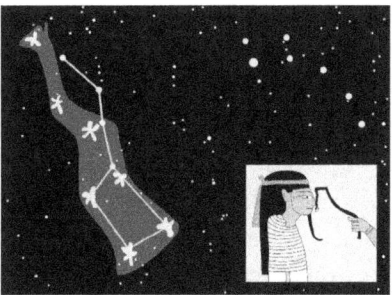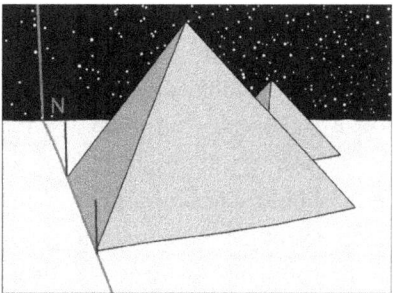

Figure 21 The Egyptians identified the group of stars in the chariot as their constellation Meskhetiu, the ox's leg. It is interesting that the ritual object, with which the mouth of the dead pharaoh was "opened," has this same shape. Two stars could have been used to identify where north was and thus orient the pyramids. Kate Spence (2000) proposes two in UMa and UMi; Juan Belmonte (2001) proposes another two.

100 today, were built from the third to the seventeenth dynasties in Egypt, although the most impressive were built in a relatively short span of time by the pharaohs of the fourth dynasty around 2500 BCE. In particular, the pharaohs Snefru, Cheops, Chephren, and Menkaure built a series of pyramids in the vicinity of their capital, Memphis, on the west bank of the Nile River. For the Egyptians, the sunset meant death, since it was the setting of their main god the Sun (Re), while in the east his birth occurred, and it was a sign of rebirth (see e.g. Belmonte & Lull 2023).

The pyramids of Egypt, especially those of this period, have practically perfect cardinal orientations. The gate of the pyramids is usually on the eastern side – that is, facing the resurrection area. However, the orientations are not entirely perfect but present a small deviation with respect to the cardinal points, and if we represent that deviation over time, we see a sequence, a correlation. This has led researchers to think that the pyramids were oriented with respect to the north, using some stars (Magli 2013).

We mentioned earlier that the stars you see in the sky facing north have an interesting peculiarity: If they are close enough to the pole, there will be a group of stars that never set or rise – the circumpolar stars. They are so named because they describe circles around the pole due to Earth's daily rotation.

For the Egyptians, these stars were of particular importance. They knew them as imperishable, and, for example, our constellation of the chariot in Ursa Major was for them the constellation of Meskhetiu, in which they identified the thigh of an ox (see Figure 21). In addition, texts tell us that when it came to orienting temples and other structures, the Egyptians had a ceremony (stretching of the cord ceremony) in which references were taken with respect to Meskhetiu.

Given this importance and what we have seen, the orientation of the pyramids is well explained by the precession of the equinoxes; their orientation is so good to the north that, for example, they used two stars of this constellation to find north (similar to how we do now to find the North Star). Due to the effect of the precession of the equinoxes, this method would vary the position of the north as determined in a systematic way over time, explaining very well what is seen (see e.g. Spence 2000; Belmonte 2001).

The important point is that simultaneous transit through the north meridian may have been used to indicate the north point, but by precession this moment changed, and thus also the exact orientation.

10 Other Ways of Measuring Orientations

We have seen that in order to determine if a given structure has a possible connection with the rise or set of any celestial object, we need three quantities: the location of the site, particularly its latitude (ϕ), the azimuth (A) of a privileged axis, and the angular elevation (altitude, h) of the horizon in the direction of the azimuth. On many occasions, we might not be able to directly get such magnitudes on site. We therefore need to devise other means to ascertain the different magnitudes.

Nowadays obtaining an accurate enough estimate of the location of a site, if we could not get this with a GPS, is rather easy with software such as Google Earth or OpenStreetMap or professional tools such as QGIS or ArcGIS.

Before moving on, we need to introduce a short explanation of how things are represented on a map. This is a representation of a part of the Earth, considered as an oblate spheroid. Flattening it onto paper (or a screen) without distortion is impossible, so cartographers use clever tricks called projections – methods for representing the curved surface of the Earth on a flat map, like the Mercator, for instance.

A particular case of this projection is the Universal Transverse Mercator, or UTM. In this system the world is sliced into sixty vertical strips called zones, each 6° of longitude wide. Each zone has its own coordinate grid, as if you wrapped a cylinder around just that slice of the Earth and then unrolled it. This projection is "transverse" because the cylinder is turned sideways, so it touches the Earth along a central meridian in that zone. Within each zone, the coordinates are given in meters (Eastings and Northings), making it very handy for measuring distances directly. The UTM minimizes distortion inside each zone, making it great for mapping and engineering work – especially if you're working over tens of kilometers, not whole continents.

Modern devices such as total stations provide direct UTM output (or national equivalents, or in a self-defined survey grid that still has a local origin and x/y axes) in centimeters. Often the grid invites interpreting the vertical lines as meridians and measuring angles from them. However, remember that the Earth is not flat and we need to correct for north angle deviation away from the zone meridian.

It is easy to see that there are two different quantities: true north, which points toward the geographic North Pole – the actual spin axis of the Earth, and grid north, the direction of the north on your UTM map grid – that is, the vertical lines on the grid. Because the Earth is curved but the grid is flat, true north and grid north are rarely the same except along the central meridian of the UTM zone. If we are located anywhere away from the grid center, because the grid is laid out as straight, parallel lines, but lines of longitude on the globe converge toward the poles, there will be a small but perceptible angular difference called grid convergence.

Normally, such value is provided in good topographic maps, and we can calculate the correction for true north (positive if grid north is east of true north, negative if west). If we have measured a bearing with respect to the grid north, we need to correct by adding or subtracting this value accordingly.

10.1 Azimuths

One of the first obvious alternatives to direct on-site measurements is by means of good site maps. Commonly, in most archaeological reports we may find detailed maps of the site, with varying details on the different structures. In most cases, we have the information of north included within the map (although we need to verify the type included, grid or true north). In those cases, the azimuth can be extracted with the aid of an angular protractor (see Figure 22).

As can be seen from Figure 22, again the most crucial part is defining the correct direction for measuring the azimuth. Once this is determined, we can obtain directly the azimuth. Of course, this measurement (as any we perform, more on this in Section 11) has an intrinsic uncertainty. The first source is the scale of our protractor. A second source is the uncertainty in the line itself. We must take all these uncertainties into account.

However, a pressing uncertainty, especially when dealing with old maps, is that on many occasions the authors do not include if the north on the map is a true north or a magnetic north, or even if it is just an approximate north direction. If the authors did include that such was a magnetic north, we can use the same tools as explained in Section 20 to determine the magnetic declination at the time of drawing the map and correct our azimuth from the magnetic declination calculated for the time when the map was created.

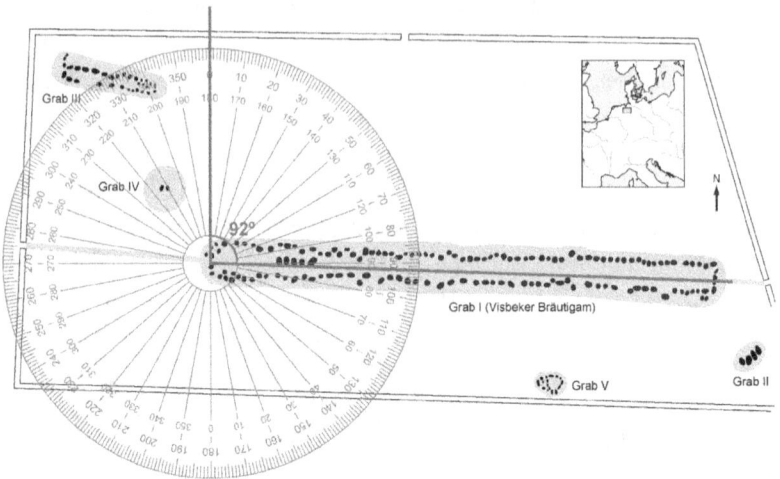

Figure 22 If we cannot take direct measurements in the field, we can refer to a good site map and the aid of a protractor. In this case, we can measure the orientation of the Visbeker Bräutigam, a megalithic tomb from northern Germany.

If we do not know if the map has true or magnetic or any other north in it, we can try to solve the measurement in the following ways. Let us imagine that we have the map, but the excavation site has been covered. If there is any remaining object depicted in the map that can still be seen aboveground (part of the wall of a house, any stelae, a path), we can try to take the measurement on site of that remain (or if this is not either possible, through satellite image; more on this on the next page) and compare it with the measurement in the map. This type of measurement would be similar to measuring the reference line indicated in Section 2 on how to do measurements with a theodolite. The difference can give us a handle on the shift that we must apply also to the orientation of the structure we are interested in.

In those cases where we do not have the possibility to go on site, or even to check if we did the measurements correctly or perhaps complete some missing data, we can refer to satellite images.

This is not the place to review the possible problems of satellite imaging. However, the main problem for us would be twofold: On the one hand, we need to make sure that the images are orthogonal. On the other, we need to establish the accuracy in the determination of the convergence angle, and how such may influence the azimuth estimates.

Commonly used geographic information system (GIS) software programs such as QGIS or ArcGIS include capabilities to estimate the azimuth of structures. Also, they include the possibility to measure azimuths from one particular point to another in an image or map and overlay images of maps within the satellite images. This makes them solid tools to obtain azimuths, also with an estimate of the associated uncertainty. These measurements can be of great value to the researcher in substitution of on-site data. Bear in mind that any of these methods is basically doing the same calculation of the reverse problem in geodetics indicated in Section 2 for the digital GPS positions. In fact, there are libraries implemented by the community to include layers to perform archaeoastronomical calculations (e,g. the QGIS EarthSunMoon plug-in to calculate Sun/Moon positions and create sunrise/sunset layers or the Azimuth & Distance / Azimuth Measurement plug-ins to make lines from azimuths and measure azimuths between points).

National geographic systems and institutes provide several online tools and geoportals to visualize and perform some basic measurements on orthographic photographs, not just satellite ones. Often these images include details that are not so clear in satellite images. And they tend to be better corrected for some of the problems of satellite images, so they appear as more suited tools to verify or extract azimuth data in many cases.

A particularly common and successful tool in the past few years has been Google Earth (GE). As this is a widely known tool and many people use it to perform a fast visualization of satellite images, I will delve a little deeper here for the explanation on how to extract the azimuth data useful in archaeoastronomy.

Let us concentrate, as a way of example, on measuring the orientation of Hatshepsut's temple at Deir el Bahari (Figure 23).

The first thing we must do is make sure we have the correct view from the top. The measurement in principle will not be affected by such, but the drawing of the line could be somehow misguided, so it is better to have these parameters locked. To do so, we can go to the view option, scroll down to the "reset" part, and there choose "inclination and orientation" to restore the north to the top and the inclination to a zenithal view.

Once this is done, GE offers a tool within the top menu to measure distances and other parameters, among which is the orientation of a given line. This is the ruler tool. If we select it, the program will open an auxiliary window with several options. The one we are interested in here is the "line." When the "ruler" is chosen, the pointer is changed to a squared target image. In this way, by clicking on top of the selected position, we can define the start and end of the line where we want to measure the orientation. In our case, we may start at the center of the top of the temple and end at the lower part of the entrance rampart.

At this moment, the auxiliary window will provide several data extracted from such line. The first is the distance as measured in the map or on the ground.

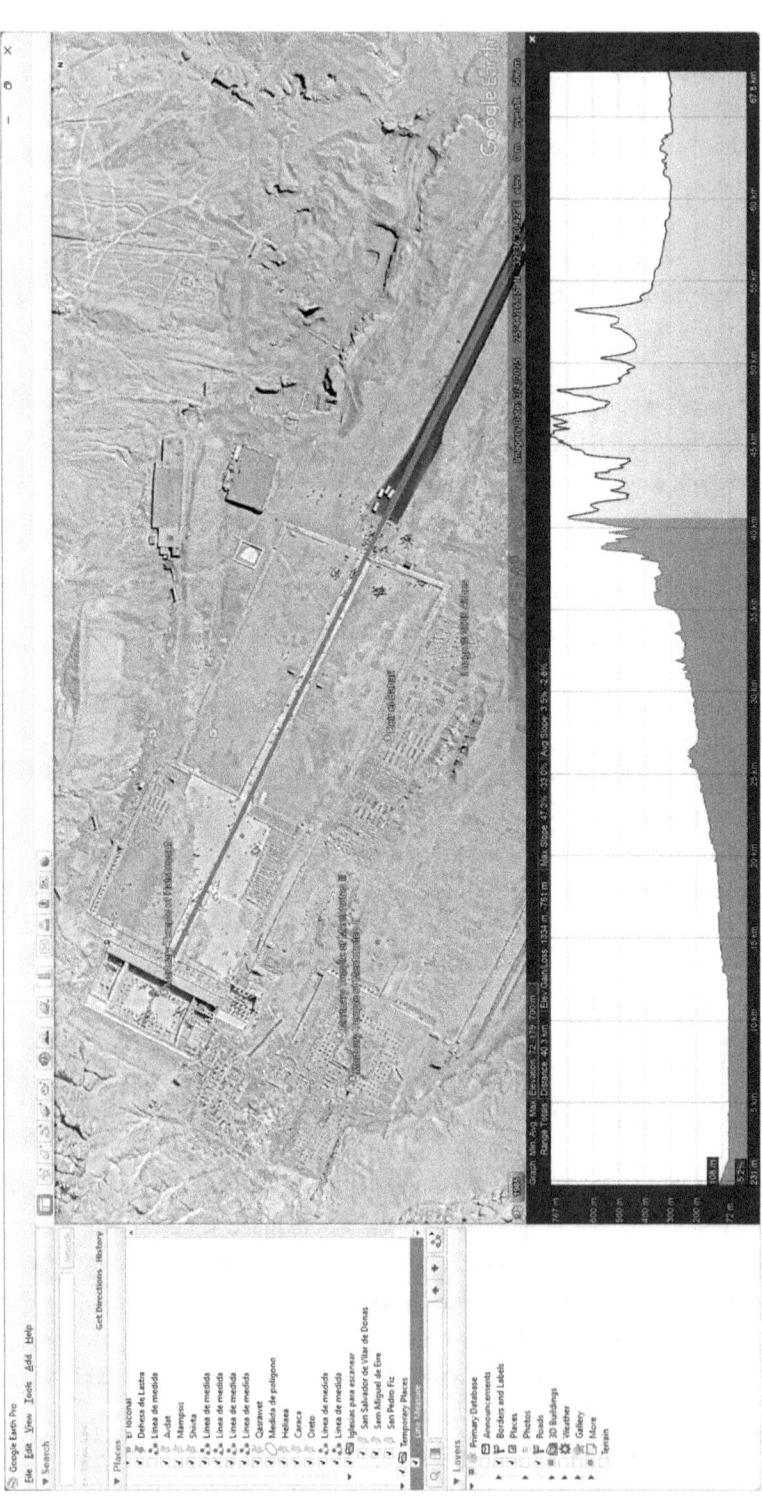

Figure 23 Screenshot of Google Earth showing the temple of Hatshepsut at Deir el Bahari. Note the thick line indicating the orientation of the temple. This has been drawn with the ruler tool (middle of the top menu). When saving the direction and choosing the option "show elevation profile," a new display appears at the bottom with the elevation profile along that line. We may then select the part that we would see from the initial point to calculate the altitude in that direction. Image courtesy of Google Earth.

Archaeoastronomy

The slight difference depends on the projection and the lenght of the line; therefore, a small discrepancy is expected. The third entry gives us the orientation with respect to north. Thus, in this way we can measure orientations in GE.

Bear in mind that this measurement has several caveats (more on this in Section 10.3), but still this is a measurement that can be used (within certain limitations) to do our archaeoastronomy work. As will be highlighted in Section 10.3, this kind of measurement should not substitute for the measurements on site, but complement them and help the researcher verify certain aspects of the measurement process.

One of the problems we can report here is that GE images are not necessarily correctly orthogonal for the site of our interest. Because they are taken from satellite images, the central part of such image will surely be nearly orthogonal, but once we move away from such a center, we can see the sides of the large buildings, as it is the case of the rampart of Hatshepsut's temple in Figure 23. Even if this is a caveat for GE images, we can try to minimize such by taking repetitive measurements at other GE images of the same site.

To do this we must profit from another of the GE tools in the upper banner. This is the "historical images" tool, with the icon of a clock and a curved arrow. By clicking on it we have the possibility to slide through previous images and see how the projection of the rampart in our case changes. The idea then would be obtaining new azimuth measurements for several of those images. It would be advisable to take at least five of these measurements, on different images, obtaining a mean of the azimuth that we will keep as the best estimate of our azimuth in this case.

10.2 Horizon Altitude

There are several instances when the horizon altitude cannot be measured on site: if the line we want to measure is blocked by trees or buildings, or if the day we do the measurements the weather is bad, and we do not have a good visibility of the horizon. In those cases, we must resort to measuring or estimating the altitude of the horizon in the lab. This could be rather more elaborate in some cases than the azimuth, but today we have several tools that help us a lot in this task.

The first method that must be mentioned is obtaining the altitude from topographic maps. If we have measured with enough accuracy the location and orientation of the site of interest, we can locate it on the map, and with the aid of a protractor and a ruler define the direction of the azimuth we have measured on site. Then we must look at the different elevation lines that our direction crosses. We then must create a graphic with distance and elevation, but we must bear in mind that the elevation we are interested is the elevation angle. Given the curvature of the Earth, we should use the following formula,

$$\tan h = \left[\frac{(E_2 - E_1)}{D} - \frac{D}{2R} \right] \tag{8}$$

where E_2 is the elevation in meters of the target location, E_1 is the elevation in meters of the origin, D is the distance in meters between points 1 and 2, and R is the radius of the Earth, also in meters (Patat 2011). In this way we may estimate h. Still, we would need to consider the effects of the atmosphere (refraction; see equation 3).

This is a rather cumbersome procedure if we need to complete it by hand. However, there are a few digital tools that we can use nowadays to speed up the process. The first one is GE. In this case, what we would need to do in GE is, after measuring the direction of interest with the ruler tool (or if we have already measured such direction on site) from the point of interest, draw a line with the same direction (azimuth) and as long as we estimate it is needed (normally a few kilometers are enough). Google Earth gives us the option in the auxiliary window to save such a line. We can do that providing an appropriate name for the line. The line will then change color. Then we should place the pointer on top of the line and by right-clicking prompt a banner with different options, where one of the last is "show elevation profile."

Clicking on it will bring up a second frame below the main one with a profile of the elevations along that line that we have drawn. We can estimate the altitudes of the two points of interest and their distances with this tool. To do so, bear in mind that the higher elevations in front of the observation point will hide the lower ones just behind them. Then we must apply formula (8) to calculate the elevation angle, the angular altitude. A similar calculation can be performed with the GIS tools such as QGIS and ArcGIS.

There are two online tools that are quite handy for estimating such elevation angles and for producing panoramic views from a given point out of Digital Terrain Models (DTMs). One is Heywhatsthat (www.heywhatsthat.com), and the other is PeakFinder (www.peakfinder.com).

Heywhatsthat takes the DTM from the radar measurements performed by a dedicated shuttle space mission (SRTM). As such the resolution of the model is variable depending on the location on Earth, but the best is up to 30 meters. Once we are on the website, we find a layout with four tabs: "All Panoramas," "View …, " "New Panorama," and "Print." To define a new panorama for our site we must navigate to "New Panorama."

On the main frame now, we can see a view into Google Maps (GM). In fact, we can choose between a map and a satellite image. In this way we can navigate to the site and, by left-clicking, select the spot we want. Then we can include a few parameters such as the height of the observer or the name of the site. And by submitting our request, in two minutes we may see a new frame with our panoramic view of the horizon from that site.

This will appear on the "View" tab. At the top we will see the panoramic view, and just below it a GM window where among other possibilities we can see where the horizon line is drawn from or the visibility cloak; these are the areas that are visible from the chosen spot. On the top frame we can move the cursor and select the azimuth of our interest by clicking. Then on the GM frame we may see where the final line of the horizon in that direction is pointing to, and just below it will appear the value of the altitude of the horizon in that direction and the distance to that most distant point.

Besides, in the frame just between the panoramic view and the GM view, we can see a profile of the terrain along that line of sight. There we may change the parameters for the visibility if we are so interested.

PeakFinder (Soldati: www.peakfinder.com) also works with DTMs, but according to its website, besides using the SRTM 30-meter model, it also includes some LiDAR terrain models in Europe from national repositories with a better resolution. PeakFinder was originally designed to facilitate the recognition of the names of mountains for hikers, but the website offers capabilities like those of HeyWhatsThat.

Here the site displays the panoramic view of a default site, with several options in the different banners. For us it is interesting that we can either introduce the coordinates of the site of interest on the search line at the top of the website, or by displaying the small map icon, we can again navigate to the site, either on a map or on a satellite image. Once the site is chosen, we select it by clicking on the bird icon. After a few seconds we can see the panoramic view in our screen.

Once this is set, we can navigate for the correct orientation, and if we click on the horizon at the desired direction, the tool provides the altitude, the elevation in meters above sea level (m.a.s.l.) and the distance to that direction.

A final general possibility we have for generating arbitrary DTM-based horizon panoramas is a dedicated software, Horizon, developed by Andrew Smith from the University of Adelaide (Australia). I will only outline here the possibilities of this program, as it has a very detailed documentation where the author describes the details with great care (www.agksmith.net/horizon).

Horizon is a bespoke software specifically built to generate panoramic views from a given location out of DTMs. The difference from the online tools just described is that it includes the possibility to mimic several astronomical phenomena at different epochs. It calculates and renders a shaded depth image (giving the impression of a 3D rendering) or a flat (2D) view of the landscape/horizon, providing a panoramic view with a grid where one can estimate and calculate positions. Besides, the user has the option to set a few lines on the sky to simulate the paths of the Sun and the Moon at chosen dates, and the brightest stars (Figure 24a).

Originally built to be used with the data from the Ordnance Survey of the UK, it can be used with the SRTM data (both the 30-meter and 90-meter accuracy data). To use these last ones, a file conversion system is included within the program, under the tools menu.

Once we have the file in the correct format, this must be loaded into the program for calculating the rendering. Then we must introduce the location of the site we want the panoramic view from. This includes subtleties such as the height of the observer, discarding data that are too close to us, or enabling, if needed, a simple vegetation model. We can set also if we want to calculate a full 3D shaded panoramic view or a flat horizon profile.

Once these options are set, and after a couple of minutes of calculations, a new window appears where we must choose the parameters of the rendering. It is here where we need to define the date for which we want the rendering to appear, the atmospheric conditions, the shading of the terrain (including date/time of solar position), astronomical positions, and the type of display. Finally, apart from a display window on our screen we can also choose to save the image as a PostScript file or as a bitmap in TIFF format.

Our display window, then, offers further calculation capabilities, such as the overall distances of the horizon. By moving the cursor on the display, we can see the azimuth on that line of sight, along with the elevation, distance to the point indicated or its height in m.a.s.l. If we are on the correct area, the direction indicated by the cursor on the horizon will also be directly translated into astronomical declination and approximate solar rising and setting dates.

A further option is the website StandingStones by David Hoyle (https://standingstones.org), that has as well the capability to show panoramic views of different stone settings in the UK and beyond.

Finally, the last program we will outline in this section is Stellarium. Stellarium is a highly versatile and complex open-source, planetarium-like computer program. It was originally intended to be used by sky lovers and amateur astronomers, but as of a few years ago it includes several capabilities well suited and specifically designed by one of its developers to be used with archaeoastronomical data (Zotti 2016).

As in the case of Horizon, I would like to make clear that these lines are by no means a substitute for the well-documented user guide of this program. I would like to encourage any potential user to follow closely the recommendations given there, as they provide a step-by-step procedure for all the capabilities I will describe.

Figure 24 (a) 3D panoramic altitude profile out of an SRTM digital terrain model produced by Horizon. The lines in the sky indicate the paths of the Sun for the solstices and equinoxes, and for the Moon at the major standstills. (b) Panoramic view of Stellarium with a panoramic view generated from PeakFinder. The lines included in the sky are part of the Archaeolines plug-in of Stellarium. (c) Panoramic photograph incorporated into Stellarium. These kinds of pictures are a perfect complement to data recording in the field.

One of the handiest capabilities in Stellarium is that it allows for the inclusion of different horizons and panoramas. This feature grants projecting a horizon profile or a panoramic view from a given site as a mask. Thus we can simulate the view of the sky from that site. The program enables us, under the correct settings, to simulate the ancient skies from nearly 13000 BCE up to the present, which is a great tool for simulating the sky at any historical (and prehistoric) time.

A note of caution should be addressed here: As in any other good planetarium program, Stellarium is reliable for the solar positions, and for stellar ones on those dates. Lunar positions for dates well into the past are less accurately calculated due to intrinsic uncertainties on the formulae that compute the Earth's rotation slowdown (the ΔT problem described in Section 7). As indicated, this is not a problem of Stellarium; it is a problem common to any of these computations. Having said that, for most applications of interest, the program is completely reliable and although problems may arise, the developers encourage any user to contact them with reported issues to solve.

The horizon to be included can be built from different sources. For example, if we have measured the complete horizon profile with a clinometer, theodolite, or total station, we may end up with a file including values of azimuth and corresponding angular elevation. Such can thus be passed on to Stellarium, under the correct format. It should be noted here that other planetarium-like programs also allow for this capability.

As indicated, in many instances we may need to resort to DTMs to produce a clean view of the horizon. In fact, the tools indicated above meanwhile include the possibility to export these files (azimuth plus altitude, or image-based panoramas).

In HWT in the "View" tab, on the right top there is a link to "In Stellarium," where we can download the polygonal horizon to be used within Stellarium.

In PeakFinder, on the left of the screen, the three horizontal lines menu opens a tab that includes the option "Export" and under this we have the possibility to export as a horizon profile for Stellarium (Figure 24b), including a collection of peak names that can also be shown in Stellarium.

Finally, also Horizon includes the possibility to save the rendering out of the DTM as a horizon profile (either as a flat horizon or as a 3D shaded rendering) for Stellarium. Note that this file needs to be included under the correct path in the Stellarium system of folders. Please refer to the Stellarium user guide for more details.

Once this is set, we can activate the horizon by looking for it on the left-hand side of the Stellarium window, under the frame "sky and viewing options window" (or pressing F4). Then a new window pops out with several tabs. One of them is the "Landscape" tab. In it, we have the different landscapes that we have in our system. Here we also have the possibility to add (or remove) landscapes, like, for instance, the ones we have downloaded from any of the programs just described. You should also activate the option "location from landscape" to utilize the coordinates stored with the landscape panorama.

Once the horizon profile is loaded, Stellarium offers a capability to measure the coordinates with our mouse. However, this is a plug-in (program extension) and therefore not one of the out-of-the-box options; to include it we must open the "Configuration window," go to plug-ins, and there search for "pointer coordinates." By selecting "Load at startup," we will have it ready for use the next time we open the program. We can then also configure which coordinates appear. Once this has been set, we will have the option as a target icon named "Show coordinates of the mouse pointer" on the panel in the lower part of the window. By selecting this option, we can use the pointer to extract azimuth and altitude values out of the horizon profile.

Stellarium is more versatile than just this kind of panoramic views out of DTMs. Another capability that is also quite handy is the possibility to upload panoramic photographs of the horizon as landscapes. A detailed tutorial on how to do this is available here: www.archeoastronomy.org/content/education/w7e991513043a000284ca32a4f03eb19.

To do this (again, for a detailed step-by-step procedure, see the user guide), we must take several photographs from the site of interest. Typically, these should be at least eight photographs that overlap reasonably (about 30 percent) between them, and that cover the whole 360° of the horizon. To do this in a proper way the best solution is to place the camera on a tripod. There are even dedicated gadgets that allow to set the number of steps to perform this. If the photographer has experience enough, she/he can do this without the aid of the tripod, although in the case of nearby important features that would shift from the slightest camera motion its use is always advisable.

Once at our desk with our series of pictures, we must combine them so that we build the panoramic view. We can do this with several different software programs, either open-source or not, such as Photoshop or GIMP. A free option is using a dedicated software called Hugin (https://hugin.sourceforge.io). Once Hugin is running on our computer, we can upload our photographs, move them to place them correctly, and build the final panoramic view in one single image.

You must make sure that the image is aligned with the azimuths and altitudes found on-site. For this, one of the artificial DTM panoramas can be included in the images as a "ground truth" against which to match the photos.

Then we must remove the sky from the final panoramic view. This can also be done either with Photoshop or GIMP. In the last one, we need to select the sky (with either the "magic" or "lasso" tool) and send the selected area to the "alpha channel." Once the whole sky is removed, we save the image (in a PNG format). Finally, we can set up a new landscape out of our images to be used in Stellarium. We can then visualize the landscape on our screen as we have done with the DTM mask (Figure 24c).

Another interesting feature of Stellarium is that we may include the paths of the Sun and Moon at interesting moments in their cycles within the sky projection. This is another plug-in, called Archaeolines, that we can set up at our convenience with a number of options that help us visualize possible connections of our landscape with particular solar and lunar configurations on the go. The user may also tune indicated lines at dedicated directions (e.g. like Mecca or Jerusalem) or toward declinations of particular stars of their choice.

Finally, Stellarium, as other engines such as Blender or Unity, allows to introduce virtual 3D models within a particular environment. For example, if we have a Greek temple or a megalithic passage tomb where we have such a virtual 3D model, Stellarium allows for its display and exploration within the planetarium software. As in the cases mentioned earlier, I will not give the details to do this in this Element. This is very well explained in the appropriate section of the Stellarium user guide. However, it might be interesting to provide a few comments on the experience of dealing with these models.

First, it should be indicated that the learning curve for implementing these models is rather steep. If you have experience in dealing with such type of data, this is going to be much easier than if you do not. Having said that, it is true that the steps to follow are rather well defined, so, once you learn you can repeat the process with minor variations at each case.

Three-dimensional virtual modeling can be a challenging process. You may start from scratch by building the 3D model with a 3D modeling tool such as SketchUp or Blender. This could be done, for example, out of the building plan of the site you want to model, for instance a church. From such, you may define in a rather smooth way the geometry of the model, and the openings (entrances, doors, windows). Then the model must be saved in Wavefront OBJ format, together with a configuration file with a few entries for Stellarium. Such file includes details on the appropriate landscape for the model setup, the coordinates of the site, and the rotation angle for the model to be facing in the right direction. Then we have our model ready. In this way, for example, we can verify the calculations performed out of our data, and in specific cases model the light and shadow interaction within buildings. It even allows for the introduction of large models (digital terrain models, DTMs) where the user can move around and see how the landscape changes and interacts with the sky on the go. An important note is that the user should be very careful with the resolution of their models, especially when trying to visualize light-and-shadow effects inside buildings, where small deviations and uncertainties may become very important in the final result.

At this point it should be indicated that although Stellarium is very well suited for these studies, especially due to the reliability of the astronomical calculations, the light-and-shadow interaction is better modeled with other engines, such as Blender or Unity, for a more realistic treatment of the light and shadows at least for current solar positions. Despite of this, the Stellarium solution is optimal for most cases. An interesting alternative, or, better, an extension, is arcAstro-VR (https://arcastrovr.org/en), where the topography of the terrain is well modeled, including terrain correction, and for modeling the sky it connects to Stellarium.

A final interesting feature of Stellarium is that it includes constellations of different cultures from around the globe. Also, users can upload from dedicated websites the ones of their choice, or even use the ones they have created.

Nowadays, 3D modeling, laser scanning, and image-based modeling, whether ground-level or airborne/drones, have both become state of the art. While an in-depth description is too much here, there are often-seen workflows in archaeological data processing (see e.g. Remondino & Campana 2014; Bosco 2022; Hostettler et al. 2024; Müster et al. 2024 for recent updates).

10.3 Digital Tools, Pros and Cons

A final tool that might be used sometimes for data collection is the smartphone. This device includes a compass and a gyroscope that combines several apps so that we can get azimuth and altitude from a site.

For instance, the app in the image uses such tools from an Android-based phone (Figure 25a). We can get a picture and then the data needed for our fieldwork can be obtained on the go.

Although, this is a very useful tool when we do not have any other of the previously indicated capabilities, it must be pointed out that it is highly inaccurate for several reasons.

Figure 25 (a) Smartphones include several apps that can be used to obtain the data needed in archaeoastronomy. In the image we show a dedicated app specifically designed to do so for Android platforms. (b) Difference between the actual horizon profile in the field and that recovered by DTMs.

The first is that the azimuth is provided by the internal compass of the phone that is very sensitive to small magnetic variations, much more than a normal compass.

The second is that the altitude of the horizon is very sensitive to the correct positioning of the phone. We must keep the phone steady in the vertical direction, or small variations to the sides might affect the final reading.

And finally, the internal gyroscope must be kept well aligned so from time to time we need to recalibrate it. This is something any user can do, but it may be time-consuming and difficult to know when such is needed.

In any case, one may think that most of these methods are indeed useful and can be an interesting alternative to fieldwork. But I'd like to remark that this is only so in those cases where such fieldwork is not possible. This is due to several reasons.

The first would be that, by only using remote sensing tools we will lose part of a fundamental information that can be gathered only by going to the field (Figure 25b). How the site relates to the environment, how it connects to other sites, or how the weather and the seasons change our perception of the site can be grasped only by going to the field.

Also, as indicated, the DTMs have a given resolution, and if the horizon is rather close to the observer, the altitude will have a large uncertainty, something that is also true, as in the previous pages, for the azimuth measurements. So it is time to delve a bit more into the uncertainties and how to deal with them.

11 Precision versus Accuracy and Error Analysis

As in any data-acquisition process, data gathering in archaeoastronomy has a number of uncertainties that we must evaluate. A correct estimation of the errors and uncertainties will result in a better knowledge of our results. This means that we have a better estimate of up to where we can trust our results.

First, as hinted several times, the first uncertainty comes from where to draw our line of interest, and how this translates into a certain direction compared with the assumed original line intended. For instance, imagine we want to measure the orientation of the corridor of a passage tomb. We may decide to measure such from the inside out, and we may decide that the line is going to be defined by the middle points of the entrance and exit of the corridor. Depending on the state of preservation of the site, this can be accurate to a few centimeters; let us, for the sake of the example, assume an accuracy of five centimeters. Now, if our corridor has a typical length of five meters, the uncertainty in our direction is given by the angle subtended by those five centimeters within the five meters. The final uncertainty is then:

$$\tan \epsilon_1 = \frac{\Delta x}{y} \tag{9}$$

Or in our example, Δx is five centimeters and y is five meters; therefore ϵ_1 is arctan(5/500). This is nearly half a degree extra of uncertainty in the midpoint of our measurements. Such would then amount to a whole degree of uncertainty extra, apart from the one derived from our measuring instrument.

This uncertainty from our particular instrument comes from the smallest number we can estimate with our measuring device. Let us assume we have measured our orientation with a magnetic compass, and we have a value of 90°. Our compass, as we have seen, has a scale with marks every degree. This means that we can estimate the reading up to $\epsilon_2 = \frac{1}{2}°$; thus our uncertainty here is of half a degree. Of course, our estimate of the heigh of the horizon will also have an uncertainty, say in this case, of 1°. Then this will translate to an uncertainty in the estimated declination and in the possible date.

Finally, a common procedure when dealing with measurement errors of this kind is to estimate the final uncertainty as the quadratic sum of these kind of uncertainties (assuming they are independent of each other):

$$\epsilon_{total}^2 = \epsilon_1^2 + \epsilon_2^2 \qquad (10)$$

A single measurement is never a good idea: We must always do several measurements of the orientation of the same building if we want to verify that we did not make a mistake in our original measurement. An interesting metaphor is that of the target and the shots (Figure 26). When we perform several measurements, we can ascertain if our measurements are accurate and precise

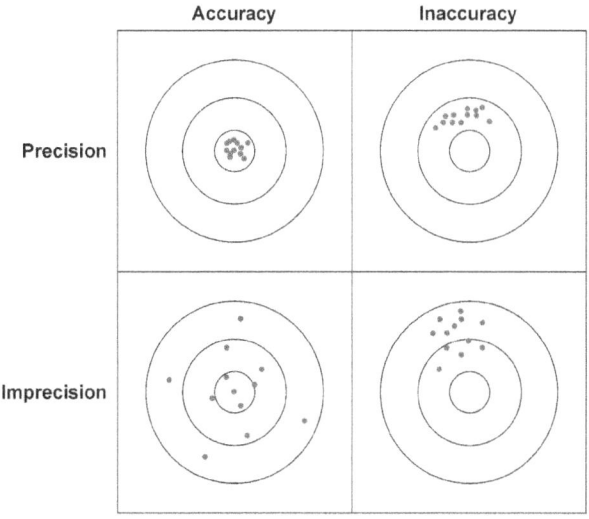

Figure 26 The target metaphor is very useful to comprehend the differences between accuracy and precision.

and quantify such deviations. This is why we must keep all measurements. Our final measured value can be estimated from these as an average (e.g. the mean or the median), while the concentration or dispersion of the data can help us evaluate the accuracy of our measurements.

In this case, as in any other measurement, the azimuth will be the mean calculated from the multiple repetitions of the measurements. And our uncertainty of the azimuth can be calculated as the squared sum of the uncertainty of each single measurement (ϵ_{total} (A)), plus the spread of the measurements indicated by the standard deviation of that mean ($\sigma(A)$):

$$\Delta \overline{A} = \sqrt{\epsilon^2(A) + \sigma^2(A)} \qquad (11)$$

One distinction we must include here is between precision and accuracy. This is clearly exemplified by the target in Figure 26. Here we can see that our shooting can be accurate when, on average, the centroid of our shots deviates little from the real target. In other words, our measurements are accurate when the average is not far from the real target. In this sense, if we have a systematic error (e.g. our peephole is slightly deviated) that may result in a systematic deviation from the real target, we can see that then our results will be inaccurate.

Apart from this, if all our shots concentrate on a small region, our shooting is very precise, while if they spread in a large area, then our shooting in imprecise. Then, to better estimate our uncertainty, we must understand our measurements and measuring devices, and estimate how accurate and precise are our measurements.

As with any derived quantity, the uncertainties in the measured quantities will translate following the derivative rules in an uncertainty in the derived declination value:

$$\Delta \delta \approx \left| \frac{\partial \delta}{\partial h} \right| \Delta h + \left| \frac{\partial \delta}{\partial A} \right| \Delta A \qquad (12)$$

In this way, we can estimate the error of our declination (δ), which is calculated through the standard spherical trigonometry formula: $\sin \delta = \cos \varphi \cos h \cos A + \sin \varphi \sin h$. The error in declination ($\Delta \delta$) is calculated by propagation through the derivative of this formula following rule (12) considering then the errors in azimuth (ΔA) and altitude (Δh), where the latitude (φ) is taken as constant.

This is then translated as follows:

$$\frac{\partial \delta}{\partial h} = \frac{\sin \varphi \cos h - \cos \varphi \cos A \sin h}{\sqrt{1 - (\sin \delta)^2}} \qquad (13)$$

$$\frac{\partial \delta}{\partial A} = \frac{-\cos \varphi \cos h \sin A}{\sqrt{1 - (\sin \delta)^2}} \tag{14}$$

It is worth noting that the error in declination would be dependent of the declination itself. It must then be recognized that such uncertainty in the declination, when it applies to the Sun, will result in an uncertainty in the dates derived. This could be estimated from the same equation of time defined in Section 4 or from the associated Table 1.

Let us investigate these equations a little longer. We can see that the uncertainty in the declination appears to be larger when we face the northern or southern most extreme positions. Why might this be?

If we remember how the lines of equal declination incline when we move away from the equator (Figures 6), we can see that for larger latitudes, the "density" of lines of equal declination in one degree of azimuth and one degree of altitude gets higher. This means that our uncertainty when we look to these directions is larger for higher latitudes than, say, closer to the equator.

This influences how we might expect to see a randomly chosen declination when we move to northern (or southern) latitudes. This can be seen in Figure 27. There we see that the uniform distribution in azimuth would translate into a bimodal distribution in declination with two maxima. These are close to the positions of the so-called accumulation points: those that will be the equivalent angle of out latitude ($\delta \sim \pm [90° - \phi]$), where these declinations are seen due north and south.

Here we have introduced a very useful tool for the interpretation of our data. We must remember these uncertainties when running toward any interpretation of our measurements.

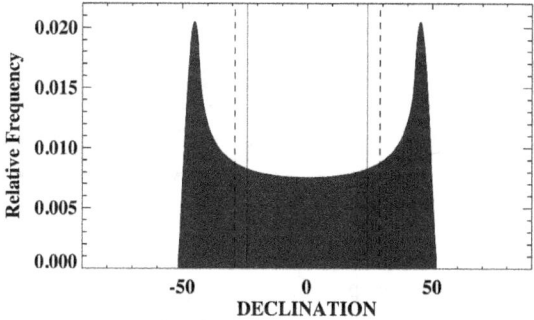

Figure 27 Declination distribution of a uniform set of orientations in azimuth for latitude 42° 30' N. These produce a bimodal graph with maxima near the so-called accumulation points, at declinations ±47.5° for that latitude.

Figure 28 Panoramic view of the skyline of Santiago de Compostela, where we can see the cathedral to the right, San Martín Pinario to the center left, and the towers of San Francisco to the extreme left. The paths of the Sun at several moments of the year are overimposed.

Let us investigate one example of such interpretation of real data. The image in Figure 28 is the view from a modern location in Santiago de Compostela in Spain. Santiago is the end of the Way of Saint James (the Camino), one of the most trotted pilgrimage routes in Europe. The skyline is dominated by the view of the Romanesque-Baroque Cathedral, where allegedly lay the remains of Apostle James. Interestingly, we can also notice two other big churches to its left. The first one is Saint Martin and the second is Saint Francis.

The figure indicates the sunrise on different dates along the year. As we can see, the Sun rises right behind the dome of the cathedral, below which is the actual tomb of the apostle, on the day of winter solstice. The second is on November 11; the Sun rises behind Saint Martin. And the final one is close to the equinox.

The relevance of these dates comes when we notice that one of the festivities associated with Saint James is celebrated on December 30 (slightly more than a week after the winter solstice), the festivity of Saint Martin is precisely celebrated by the Catholic Church on November 11, and that of Saint Francis is celebrated on October 4 (the autumn equinox is on September 22).

Thus we could advance a tentative hypothesis that the chosen backsight is on a very relevant position within the landscape of Santiago, especially when we realize that this is the house of an archaeoastronomer! Is there anything to this?

Well, I am afraid this is a typical example of overinterpretation. The problem is manyfold: First, we are guiding our eye because we are archaeoastronomers, and as humans we tend to see patterns in many places. To try to minimize this problem, we must first try to be fair to the data. To do this we must recognize that, given the size of the buildings, the number of days the Sun will rise behind each building is going to be large, so it is no surprise that on some of them there is a significant event related to the saints venerated in these churches.

Archaeoastronomy

This can be somehow quantified by an estimate of the probability that at least these three directions are connected to relevant items for us. This is done with the formula of chance alignment – that is, we have a number of directions, and we want to know if their possible astronomical alignment could be fortuitous.

The probability P to hit at least r targets in n directions is (Ruggles 1999),

$$P = 1 - \sum_{s=0}^{r-1} \frac{n!}{s!(n-s)!} p^s (1-p)^{n-s} \qquad (15)$$

where p is the portion of the horizon covered by our targets, or the uncertainty in our measurements. The capital sigma implies that we must do a summation of r elements, over all the values of s, from 0 to $r-1$.

The meaning of this is that the smaller the value of P the smaller the probability that the alignment is by chance. But even if P is very small, we cannot ascertain that the alignment is intentional, but we can discard the chance alignment with a larger confidence.

One of the key aspects to apply the formula is estimating p, the portion of the horizon that we will consider a hit for the target. In this calculation the estimate of the uncertainty is of key importance, but also our level of expected accuracy. This means that even if we measured the orientation with a given precision (see Section 11), we may estimate that this value is rather small. But we must also estimate here what is the level of accuracy we assume to be a hit: For example, if we have measured the orientation such that the azimuth is 120° with an uncertainty of ± 1°, this may be off the winter solstice direction (imagine this is 122°). However, we may estimate that given the state of preservation of the remains measured and the accuracy expected by the building, we may assume that we have a hit if we are away from this 122° value by less than 2°, or even cruder estimates. This must always be estimated ahead of any calculation to be fair to the data, as indicated.

Another issue is the number of potential targets to consider. We must not consider the targets only as a function of the data, because then we can fall into circularity issues. Again, this should be done before any data are obtained, if possible.

Another fundamental aspect is estimating the number of total possibilities (n). This again should include not only the possible astronomical ones but any that might potentially have given any other target, like topographic ones, for example. And finally, we need the number of hits in the alleged targets (r).

Now, if we apply this to the example in Santiago, here I have a view of nearly 180° of the horizon; the rest is blocked by a nearby hill. This is the total amount of horizon I will consider here. Although, we have measured the orientations with a rather crude accuracy, as the one of 1°, we must take into consideration that each building is covering a large part of the horizon: the cathedral nearly 10°, Saint Martin, another 15° and Saint Francis, 10°. There is a fourth possible target, the church of Santa Susana, that we must include in our calculations. Besides, it is in the solar range, but although the Sun rises behind this church, the corresponding dates do not match the patron saint's feast day. This church only subtends 3° in the horizon. Now, as we are considering only a fraction of the horizon where the sun rises, for the latitude of Santiago, this is nearly 66°.

Then our value for $p = (10+15+10+3)/66 = 0.58$. the value n in our case is 4, and we have three hits on targets. With these values, from formula (15) we can see that the probability $P = 0.74$. As we can observe, this is a large probability. In fact, this is larger than the probability of having a head after tossing a coin (0.5) and guessing the result, so we cannot discard the chance alignment in our case.

Besides all the intrinsic errors of the measuring device, we must remember that we are observing the astronomical phenomena through the atmosphere, which introduces several uncertainties. Therefore, we may estimate the best determination of the position on the horizon of singular celestial bodies using either a measuring instrument or the naked eye; instrumental methods – when atmospheric refraction is modeled with accurate local soundings – can yield precision better than 0.01" up to ~70° zenith, degrading to ~10" at the horizon, whereas unaided visual estimates may suffer errors of several arcminutes to degrees depending on atmospheric conditions (Kurzynska 1987; Corbard et al. 2018).

When we take the size of the object, its brightness, and the atmospheric effects into account, the accuracy in the settings can be estimated, depending on conditions, between 80 percent and 100 percent of the figures indicated in Table 4. The values are given for latitudes typical of Mediterranean cultures, but we can deduce from them that the higher the latitude we will have even greater uncertainty. As can be seen, it is difficult to predict the position of the

Table 4 Intrinsic uncertainty due to atmospheric effects

Phenomenon	30°N	30°N with	40°N	40°N with
Solstice	1° 12'	0° 30'	1° 36'	0° 42'
Lunastice	1° 12'	0° 42'	1° 42'	1° 06'
Sirius or Venus	0° 54'	0° 36'	1° 12'	0° 48'
Pleiades	3° 12'	2° 30'	4° 36'	3° 42'

sunrise at the solstice with a better accuracy than the diameter of the Sun (32'), being even worse in the case of lunar observations. The data from Sirius and Venus are useful for any star or planet of zero or negative magnitude, as they are supposed to be visible from the moment of their rise above mathematical horizon.

Something that can be deduced immediately from this table is that using star alignments to date monuments is completely unfounded unless additional information is available from documentary sources or archaeological evidence.

11.1 One Swallow Does Not a Summer Make

In many cases, we may estimate the probability in the way indicated, but on several occasions, we will not have enough confidence with one case to know if the alignment we have was intentional. In all cases, it is worth trying to obtain further contextual information from the archaeological record or other cultural remains that may inform us of the relevance of such orientation.

For example, in the case of the spot in Santiago, the cultural case was apparently clear, but the hypothesis that the place had to be of relevance was based on flawed reasoning, and there is nothing relevant in the spot where the observation was made. And this is also of key importance: Is the backsight (the observation point) of any relevance?

In any case, in several other instances, it will be wise to compare our data with other similar cases. We can try thus to find whether with more observations, a pattern shows up, a repetition of the targets observed.

In such cases we can do basic statistical studies to verify if there is a relevant orientation out of a statistically significant sample of observations. For example, in southern Spain and central Portugal, there are nearly 200 megalithic tombs, all of them of very similar typology, material remains, and chronology, in a wide area, of nearly 100 by 100 square kilometers (Hoskin 2015). These megalithic monuments, dated from the fourth millennium BCE, are formed by an octagonal chamber, with seven sides occupied by orthostats, and the eight leading toward a megalithic corridor that forms the entrance to the tomb. The orientations and altitudes of all those that were in a good state of preservation have been measured (Hoskin 2001; Figure 29a).

When comparing these many orientations, a first insight comes by employing some basic statistical tools. Thus we can see that all of them are facing sunrise at some moment along the year. In this case, and with such consistency, we can be rather sure that there is an intentionality behind that can be linked to an astronomical target.

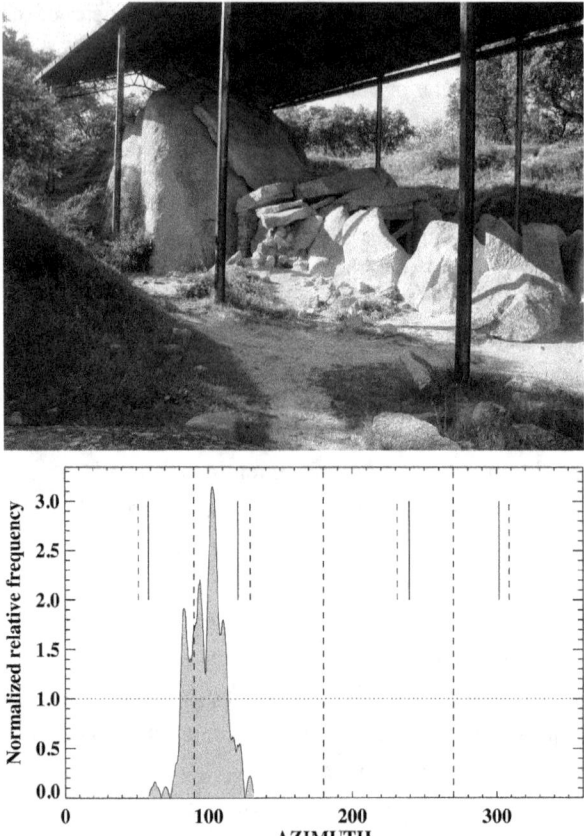

Figure 29 (a) Anta Grande do Zambujeiro, anta of seven orthostats in the chamber, with an entrance corridor. Located near Évora (Portugal; photo: A. C. González). (b) Histogram of orientations (azimuths) for the dolmens of the Alentejo (Portugal; data from Hoskin 2001). Vertical lines indicate the extremes of sunrise and sunset of the Sun (short solid) and the moon (short dashed), as well as the cardinal points (long dashed).

A statistical study is of paramount importance when we do not have texts, as in this case, that guide us when it comes to glimpsing the motivations for choosing a certain orientation for a monument. If instead of a single monument we have a large number that repeat that orientation in a more or less coherent way, that is telling us that the orientation is not random but that there was a reason to choose it.

Returning to the case of the Alentejo dolmens, the average of the orientations occurs for azimuth of 98.8°, with generally low horizon altitudes (less than 1°). The standard deviation is 17.5°, which tells us that the concentration around the mean value is high. One way to visualize this is by using a histogram. A histogram tells us for each value of a given quantity (e.g. azimuth) how many subjects in our sample have that value.

A histogram is however a rather crude representation, as we include all values within the same box, regardless of the information we have about them. One way to overcome this situation is by employing a density distribution (kernel density estimate, or KDE). This assumes that each of our measurements can be modeled by a small distribution function, a Gaussian, for example (although others might work better). In this case, the mean value of the Gaussian would be our measurement for the orientation, while the spread of the Gaussian will be our uncertainty estimate. The resultant figure is similar to the histogram with a softer appearance, often named a curvigram (see e.g. Figure 29b).

If we make this representation for the dolmens of the Alentejo (Figure 29b) and include in this representation the azimuth values of the extreme positions of the Sun for the time they were built, we see that they are all within those limits. This already confirms that a solar orientation is highly plausible, perhaps toward sunrise at the time of the construction of the tomb. We also see that a large part of the orientations appears around azimuths close to 90°, which could be associated with the equinoxes. As we saw before, this point is when the Sun crosses the celestial equator and its $\delta = 0°$.

Now a different and more cumbersome task is assigning the target and trying to grasp the meaning, the intent, behind such patterns. To do this, again we must take the overall contextual (cultural) information into account.

What could have been the motivation for this orientation? Perhaps a ritual involved the equinox. An average orientation at values of 98° tells us that it was possibly oriented either before the spring equinox or after the autumn equinox. Considering the tasks of a society based on agriculture and livestock, it seems that the orientation toward dates after the autumn equinox may be logical, given that is when the harvest and work in the fields ends, and even today in many towns and cities in the area festivals are celebrated at that time (Saint Matthew).

A useful tool to compare our data with is knowing what the expected solar and lunar distributions would be for one year. These are given in Figure 30 and we can explore such to develop our hypothesis further. An interesting exercise is to compare these distributions with the movements of the Sun and the Moon seen in Videos 1 and 2.

12 Conclusion

Archaeoastronomy provides us with very useful information about specific aspects of the culture of past peoples. In particular, it can be appreciated that

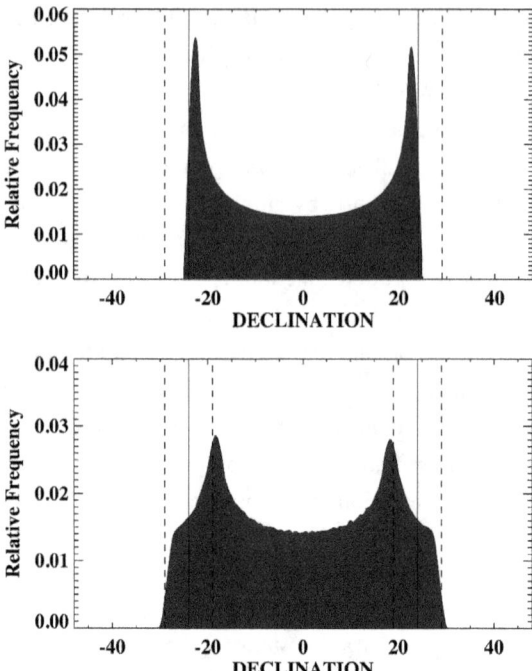

Figure 30 (a) Expected distribution of a uniform orientation population within the solar movements in the horizon. Vertical solid lines are the solar limits, while vertical dashed lines are the lunar limits. (b) Same as before but for the Moon.

the orientation and location of built structures may give us insight into very specific notions of past societies, such as the concepts of space and, when such is correlated with the heavenly cycles, the concept of time.

Both of them also may be linked to aspects of the ritual domain, either by way of the importance the societies provided to these places, and times of gathering, or by the histories they incorporated as explanations for the events happening.

Indeed the theoretical approaches to dig further into such implications and interpretations are beyond the scope of this Element. Of course, this Element only aims to give some guidelines and an introduction to the topic on how to properly obtain the data in the field or in the laboratory. Researchers in the field have developed a number of analytical techniques that may help the user further extract possible relations from these data. Such may include the use of different mathematical and statistical techniques. This would be the scope of a further volume devoted to the analysis of the archaeoastronomical data by employing commonly used software and websites developed by the author and his collaborators.

References

Belmonte, J. A. 2001. On the Orientation of the Old Kingdom Pyramids. *Archaeoastronomy* 26: S1–20.

Belmonte, J. A. 2015. Ancient "Observatories": A Relevant Concept? in C. L. N. Ruggles, (ed.) *Handbook of Archaeoastronomy and Ethnoastronomy*. New York: Springer, 133–146.

Belmonte, J. A. & J. Lull. 2023. *Astronomy of Ancient Egypt: A Cultural Perspective*. Cham: Springer.

Belmonte, J. A. & M. Shaltout (eds.). 2009. *In Search of Cosmic Order: Selected Essays on Egyptian Archaeoastronomy*. Cairo: Supreme Council of Antiquities Press.

Bender, B. 1998. *Stonehenge: Making Space*. Leamington Spa: Berg.

Bosco, A. 2022. *3D Surveying Methods and Digital Information Management for Archaeological Heritage*. Oxford: BAR Publishing. https://doi.org/10.30861/9781407359731.

Cohen, M. E. 1993. *Cultic Calendars of the Ancient Near East*. Bethesda, MD: CDL Press.

Corbard, T., R. Ikhlef, F. Morand, M. Meftah & C. Renaud. 2018. On the Importance of Astronomical Refraction for Modern Solar Astrometric Measurements. *Monthly Notices of the Royal Astronomical Society* 483(3): 3865–3877.

Criado Boado, F. 2012. *Arqueológicas: La razón perdida*. Barcelona: Bellaterra.

Cruz, J., J. Cortés, C. Yufla & N. Henríquez. 2013. Palabras de las Autoras. In *Atacameño Ethnoastronomy Project: The Universe of Our Elders*. Online document: www.almaobservatory.org/es/publications/el-universo-de-nuestros-abuelos, pp. 15–35. Last accessed October 19, 2021.

Darvill, T. 2022. Keeping Time at Stonehenge. *Antiquity* 76: 319–335.

Da Silva, C. M. 2004. The Spring Full Moon. *Journal for the History of Astronomy* 25: 475–478.

Flanders, T. & P. J. Creed. 2008. Transparency and Atmospheric Extinction. *Sky & Telescope*. June 10. https://skyandtelescope.org/astronomy-resources/transparency-and-atmospheric-extinction. Last accessed August 8, 2025.

Fletcher, M. & G. R. Lock. 2005. *Digging Numbers: Elementary Statistics for Archaeologists*. Oxford: Oxford University School of Archaeology Monographs.

García Quintela, M. & A. C. González-García. 2009. Arqueoastronomía, antropología y paisaje. *Complutum* 20(2): 39–54.

Gell, A. 1992. *The Anthropology of Time*. London: Berg.

González-García, A. C. 2013. Profiting from Models of Astronomical Alignments to Unveil Ancient Cosmologies in Europe and the Mediterranean. *Anthropological Notebooks* 19(Supplement): 49–68.

González-García, A. C. 2024. Traveling between Natural and Human Sciences. A Professional Voyage toward Cultural Astronomy, in T. Wynn, K. A. Overmann & F. L. Coolidge (eds.) *The Oxford Handbook of Cognitive Archaeology*. Oxford: Oxford University Press, 1005–1018.

González-García, A. C. & J. A. Belmonte. 2006. Which Equinox? Archaeoastronomy. *Journal of Astronomy in Culture* 20: 95–107.

González-García, A. C. & J. A. Belmonte. 2019. Archaeoastronomy: A Sustainable Way to Grasp the Skylore of Past Societies. *Sustainability* 11(8): 2240. https://doi.org/10.3390/su11082240.

González-García, A. C., M. V. García Quintela & J. A. Belmonte. 2016. Landscape Construction and Time Reckoning in Iron Age Celtic Iberia. *Documenta Praehistorica*, 43: 479–498.

Green, R. M. 1985. *Spherical Astronomy*. Cambridge: Cambridge University Press.

Hannah, R. 2005. *Greek and Roman Calendars*. London: Duckworth.

Hawkins, G. S. 1965. *Stonehenge Decoded*. London: Doubleday & Company.

Hodder, I. 1982. *The Present Past*. Barnsley: Pen & Sword Books

Hoskin, M. 2001. *Tombs, Temples and Their Orientations: New Perspectives in Mediterranean Prehistory*. Bognor Regis: Ocarina.

Hoskin, M. 2015. Seven-Stone Antas, in C. L. N. Ruggles (ed.) *Handbook of Archaeoastronomy and Ethnoastronomy*. New York: Springer, 1149–1152.

Hostettler, M., A. Buhlke, C. Drummer, L. Emmenegger, J. Reich & C. Stäheli. 2024. *The 3 Dimensions of Digitalised Archaeology*. Springer, Cham.

Ingold, T. 1993. The Temporality of the Landscape. *World Archaeology* 25(2): 152–174.

Iwaniszewski, S. 2009. Por una astronomía cultural renovada. *Complutum* 20(2): 23–37.

Iwaniszewski, S. 2021. Archaeoastronomical Sites as Fields of Relationship, in A. C. González-García, R. M. Frank, L. D. Sims, M. A. Rappenglück, G. Zotti, J. A. Belmonte & I. Sprajc (eds.) *Beyond Paradigms in Cultural Astronomy*. BAR International Series 3033. Oxford: BAR Publishing, 74–80.

Jacobson, M. 1993. *Foundations of Neuroscience*. New York: Springer.

Karttunen H., P. Kröger, H. Oja, M. Poutanen & K. J. Donner. 2003. *Fundamental Astronomy*. New York: Springer.

Krupp, E. C. 1997. Archaeoastronomy, in J. Lankford (ed.) *History of Astronomy, an Encyclopedia*. New York: Routledge, 21–30.

Kurziynska, K. 1987. Precision in Determination of Astronomical Refraction from Aerological Data. *Astronomische Nachrichten* 308(5): 323–328.

Magli, G. 2013. *Architecture, Astronomy and Sacred Landscape in Ancient Egypt*. Cambridge: Cambridge University Press.

Magli, G. 2020. *Archaeoastronomy: Introduction to the Science of Stars and Stones*. Cham: Springer Nature.

Magli, G. & J. A. Belmonte. 2023. Archaeoastronomy and the Alleged "Stonehenge Calendar." *Antiquity* 97(393): 745–751.

Massey, D. 2006. Landscape as a Provocation. *Journal of Material Culture* 11: 33–48.

Meeus, J. 1991. *Astronomical Algorithms*. Richmond, VA: William-Bell.

Müster, S. et al. 2024. *Handbook of Digital 3D Reconstruction of Historical Architecture*. Cham: Springer.

Parker-Pearson, M. 2012. *Stonehenge: Exploring the Greatest Stone Age Mystery*. London: Simon & Schuster.

Patat, F. 2011. Horizon Synthesis for Archaeo-astronomical Purposes. *Astronomische Nachrichten* 332(7): 743–749. https://doi.org/10.1002/asna.201111570.

Prendergast, F. 2015. Techniques of Field Survey, in C. L. N. Ruggles (ed.) *Handbook of Archaeoastronomy and Ethnoastronomy*. New York: Springer, 389–410.

Rappenglück, M. A. 2013. Astro-Maniacs: Methodological Concepts of Cultural Astronomy Focused on Case Studies of Earlier Prehistory. *Anthropological Notebooks* 19(Supplement): 83–100.

Rappenglück, M. A. 2021. How Do We Know What They Were Thinking? Archaeoastronomy between Science and Speculation: Paleolithic Case Studies. Archaeoastronomical Sites as Fields of Relationship, in A. C. González-García, R. M. Frank, L. D. Sims, M. A. Rappenglück, G. Zotti, J. A. Belmonte & I. Sprajc (eds.) *Beyond Paradigms in Cultural Astronomy*. BAR International Series 3033: 65–73.

Remondino, F. & Campana, S. 2014. *3D Recording and Modelling in Archaeology and Cultural Heritage Theory and Best Practices*. BAR International Series S2598.

Ruggles, C. L. N. 1997a. Astronomy and Stonehenge. *Proceedings of the British Academy* 92: 203–229.

Ruggles, C. L. N. 1997b. Whose Equinox? *Archaeoastronomy* 22: S45–50.

Ruggles, C. L. N. 1999. *Astronomy in Prehistoric Britain and Ireland*. New Haven, CT: Yale University Press.

Ruggles, C. L. N. 2011. Pushing Back the Frontiers or Still Running Around the Same Circles? Interpreting "Archaeoastronomy" Thirty Years On, in C. L. N. Ruggles (ed.) *Archaeoastronomy and Ethnoastronomy: Building Bridges across Cultures*. IAU Symposium 178. Cambridge: Cambridge University Press, 1–18.

Ruggles, C. L. N. & A. Chadburn. 2024. *Stonehenge: Sighting the Sun*. Historic England.

Scarre, C. 2002. Coast and Cosmos: The Neolithic Monuments of Northern Brittany, in C. Scarre (ed.) *Monuments and Landscape in Atlantic Europe: Perception and Society during the Neolithic and Early Bronze Age*. London: Routledge, 84–102.

Schaefer, B. 1993. Astronomy and the Limits of Vision. *Vistas in Astronomy* 36: 311–361.

Silva, F. & F. Pimenta. 2012. The Crossover of the Sun and the Moon. *Journal for the History of Astronomy* xliii: 191–208.

Sims, L. D. 2007. The Solarization of the Moon: Manipulated Knowledge at Stonehenge. *Cambridge Archaeological Journal* 16(2): 191–207.

Smith, A. G. K. 2020. Horizon User Guide and Implementation Notes. Documentation Version 0.16. January 1. www.agksmith.net/horizon.

Spence, K. 2000. Ancient Egyptian Chronology and the Astronomical Orientation of Pyramids. *Nature* 408: 320–324.

Sprajc, I. 1996. *Venus, Lluvia, Maiz: Simbolismo y astronomía en la religión Mesoamericana*. Mexico: Instituto Nacional de Antropología e Historia.

Stern, S. 2012. *Calendars in Antiquity: Empires, States and Societies*. Oxford: Oxford University Press.

Tilley, C. 1996. *A Phenomenology of Landscape*. Oxford: Berg.

Zotti, G. 2016. Open-Source Virtual Archaeoastronomy. *Mediterranean Archaeology and Archaeometry* 16: 17–24.

Cambridge Elements

Current Archaeological Tools and Techniques

Hans Barnard
Cotsen Institute of Archaeology

Hans Barnard was associate adjunct professor in the Department of Near Eastern Languages and Cultures as well as associate researcher at the Cotsen Institute of Archaeology, both at the University of California, Los Angeles. He currently works at the Roman site of Industria in northern Italy and previously participated in archaeological projects in Armenia, Chile, Egypt, Ethiopia, Italy, Iceland, Panama, Peru, Sudan, Syria, Tunisia, and Yemen. This is reflected in the seven books and more than 100 articles and chapters to which he contributed.

Willeke Wendrich
Polytechnic University of Turin

Willeke Wendrich is Professor of Cultural Heritage and Digital Humanities at the Politecnico di Torino (Turin, Italy). Until 2023 she was Professor of Egyptian Archaeology and Digital Humanities at the University of California, Los Angeles, and the first holder of the Joan Silsbee Chair in African Cultural Archaeology. Between 2015 and 2023 she was Director of the Cotsen Institute of Archaeology, with which she remains affiliated. She managed archaeological projects in Egypt, Ethiopia, Italy, and Yemen, and is on the board of the International Association of Egyptologists, Museo Egizio (Turin, Italy), the Institute for Field Research, and the online UCLA Encyclopedia of Egyptology.

About the Series

Cambridge University Press and the Cotsen Institute of Archaeology at UCLA collaborate on this series of Elements, which aims to facilitate deployment of specific techniques by archaeologists in the field and in the laboratory. It provides readers with a basic understanding of selected techniques, followed by clear instructions how to implement them, or how to collect samples to be analyzed by a third party, and how to approach interpretation of the results.

Cambridge Elements =

Current Archaeological Tools and Techniques

Elements in the Series

Mobile Landscapes and Their Enduring Places
Bruno David, Jean-Jacques Delannoy and Jessie Birkett-Rees

Cultural Burning
Bruno David, Michael-Shawn Fletcher, Simon Connor, Virginia Ruth Pullin, Jessie Birkett-Rees, Jean-Jacques Delannoy, Michela Mariani, Anthony Romano, S. Yoshi Maezumi

Knowledge Discovery from Archaeological Materials
Pedro A. López García, Denisse L. Argote, Manuel A. Torres-García, Michael C. Thrun

Machine Learning for Archaeological Applications in R
Denisse L. Argote, Pedro A. López-García, Manuel A. Torres García, Michael C. Thrun

Worked Bone, Antler, Ivory, and Keratinous Materials
Adam DiBattista

Infrared Spectroscopy of Archaeological Sediments
Michael B. Toffolo

Retrospective and Prospective for Scientific Provenance Studies in Archaeology
Mark Pollard

Archaeological Wood and Woodworking
Caroline Arbuckle MacLeod

Bioarchaeology of Infants and Children
L. Creighton Avery

Ceramic Analysis: Laboratory Methods
Irmgard Hein, Mustafa Kibaroğlu, Michaela Schauer, Anno Hein, Georgios Polymeris, Judit Molera, Trinitat Pradell

Determining Provenance from Compositional Data
Pedro A. López-García, Denisse L. Argote

Archaeoastronomy: Data Collection and Analysis
A. César González-García

A full series listing is available at: www.cambridge.org/EATT